MO[DERN]
WOOL

12 Appliqué Projects to Get You Stitching

Tonya Alexander

stashBOOKS®

an imprint of C&T Publishing

April 27.1996

Text copyright © 2021 by Tonya Alexander

Photography and artwork copyright © 2021 by C&T Publishing, Inc.

Publisher: Amy Barrett-Daffin

Creative Director: Gailen Runge

Acquisitions Editor: Roxane Cerda

Managing Editor: Liz Aneloski

Editor: Kathryn Patterson

Technical Editors: Linda Johnson and Debbie Rodgers

Cover/Book Designer: April Mostek

Production Coordinator: Tim Manibusan

Production Editor: Alice Mace Nakanishi

Illustrators: Linda Johnson and Kristyne Czepuryk

Photo Assistant: Lauren Herberg

Photography by Estefany Gonzalez of C&T Publishing, Inc.,
unless otherwise noted

Published by Stash Books, an imprint of C&T Publishing, Inc., P.O. Box 1456,
Lafayette, CA 94549

Library of Congress Cataloging-in-Publication Data

Names: Alexander, Tonya, 1969- author.

Title: Modern wool : 12 appliqué projects to get you stitching /
Tonya Alexander.

Description: Lafayette, CA : Stash Books, [2021] | Includes
bibliographical references.

Identifiers: LCCN 2020046845 | ISBN 9781644030738
(trade paperback) | ISBN 9781644030745 (ebook)

Subjects: LCSH: Appliqué--Patterns. | Wool fabrics.

Classification: LCC TT779 .A396 2021 | DDC 746.44/5041--dc23

LC record available at https://lccn.loc.gov/2020046845

Printed in the USA

10 9 8 7 6 5 4 3 2 1

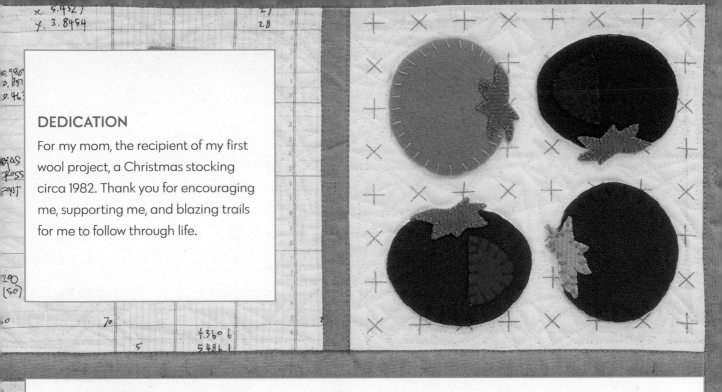

DEDICATION

For my mom, the recipient of my first wool project, a Christmas stocking circa 1982. Thank you for encouraging me, supporting me, and blazing trails for me to follow through life.

ACKNOWLEDGMENTS

A book often begins with the author's dream, but it takes a team to bring it into reality and to make it the best that it can be. This is definitely true for *Modern Wool*. I would like to especially thank:

- The team at C&T Publishing, for not only entertaining my wool project dream, but for making it come true. Thank you for welcoming me into the C&T family. Thanks to Roxane Cerda, for her vision and boldness; Liz Aneloski and Kathy Patterson, for editorial expertise; Linda Johnson and Debbie Rodgers, for much needed and much appreciated technical editing; all the members of the creative team that brought these projects to life in this beautiful book; and the business team working to take it out into the real world.

- Tracey Fisher and Nikki Crisp, for their beautiful skills in professional longarm quilting, their creativity and partnership in my projects, their encouragement, and most importantly, for being my friends.

- The following companies for providing excellent products for use in my projects: Andover Fabrics, Hobbs Batting, Local Farm Girl, and National Nonwovens.

- Last but not least, my family, above all my husband, John, who patiently supports me as I disappear into my studio to work on this project and many others and takes care of the details of life so that I can.

CONTENTS

Light and dark

COLORWAYS!

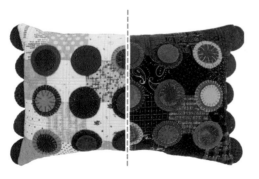

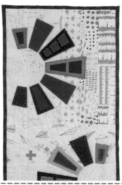

INTRODUCTION

Beautiful, forgiving, mobile, satisfying—just some of the qualities I love most about wool hand-appliqué projects. And while all these things are true of wool appliqué, the colors and projects that come to mind have traditionally tended to be darker and more homespun in appearance which would seem at odds with the general aesthetic commonly associated with more modern quilting styles. But I believe the two are not mutually exclusive. There is more, so much more, out there for contemporary quilters to experience in the joy and satisfaction of working with wool. And so here we are, *Modern Wool*. My quilt designs have always been based on traditional quilt blocks and techniques and these projects are no different. What is different are the combinations and design choices we'll make to bring our wool appliqué to a different place. My hope is that this place is one that is approachable and enjoyable for every skill level and style of quilter.

FABRICS

Wool Options

For something so seemingly straightforward, wool appliqué gets complicated immediately with two simple words: *wool* and *felt* and their combinations. Wool felt, felted wool, pre-felted wool, craft felt, non-felting wool, and the list goes on. So, what are we talking about here?

First, let's narrow our choices. For wool appliqué projects, you will want to choose felted wool or quality wool felt typically carried in quilt shops. Craft felt you find in the aisles of the craft store has other applications, but is not the best choice for wool appliqué.

FELTED WOOL

Felted wool, or basic wool fabric that you find in quilt shops, is just that—actual fabric made from wool. Fibers are spun into threads that are then woven into fabric—just like cotton quilting fabrics, except using a wool fiber instead of a cotton fiber. Once the wool fibers are woven to create the wool fabric, it can then be felted, a process of washing and drying the wool fabric with high heat. Felting fluffs up the fibers that give wool fabric its recognizable soft, fuzzy quality. The more it is felted, the fuzzier if can appear.

Felted wool has a wonderful, soft feel, or what's referred to in fabric as *hand*. Being a natural fiber is what makes wool a great choice for custom hand-dyed applications. It takes and holds dyes beautifully and can produce intense saturated solids as well as limitless unique mottled color variations that are the hallmark of custom hand-dyed fabrics. Because fabric dyeing processes can vary widely to create such a variety of colors and textures, it is important to check for colorfastness in felted wool before using it in our projects.

> ### *Repurposing Wool from Old Clothing*
>
> You can repurpose wool from old clothing and even do your own overdyeing to experiment with colors. The challenge is determining what kind of wool fabric was used in its construction.
>
> Non-felting wool fabric, often used for clothing, is manufactured specifically not to felt. No matter how much you continue to wash and dry it, it will maintain its appearance. There's really no good way to tell if non-felting wool fabric was used in a garment (unless the label specifically says so) other than to try to felt it and test the result.
>
> To felt new unfelted wool fabric off the bolt or repurposed wool fabric from old clothing, wash in the hot cycle of a washing machine with an agitator. Dry on high heat. You can also throw a couple of tennis balls in the dryer with the fabric to aid in the felting process. You can choose to deconstruct the fabric pieces from clothing before or after washing and drying.

Felted wool is supple and is suited to almost any shape or curve in appliqué. It can be stitched in a way to make the stitches sink in and almost disappear. Wool is very forgiving, and these are qualities that make wool appliqué perfect for beginners or for relaxing stitching for any skill level.

● **TIP** *Testing for Color Bleeding*
To test for color bleeding in your wool fabrics, wet a corner or scrap piece of the wool with warm or hot water. Blot between two pieces of scrap white or muslin fabric and press with a hot iron to see if the color bleeds onto the lighter fabrics. If it does bleed, prewash your wool. Include a color catcher sheet (found in the laundry aisle of the grocery or home goods store) in the washing machine, and test again after drying before using in your project construction.

WOOL FELT

The other option is wool felt. Wool felt is also made using wool fibers, or sometimes a blend of fibers, but instead of being woven into fabric, the fibers are compressed under a high heat manufacturing process to create a new product, felt. Both felt and fabric are made with varying amounts of the same raw material, but they have different properties. Wool felt is a denser, and in some ways more stable, product. A cut made through wool felt produces a clean, crisp edge. By its very construction, wool felt does not fray when used for appliqué.

Wool felt can have a very different feel or hand than felted wool. The colors available are clear, true, and typically colorfast, and hand stitching stays more on the surface of the wool felt instead of sinking down into the fabric.

Personal preferences factor in. What the fabric feels like to work with and how it performs and appears in the final project are probably the biggest reasons quilters choose one over the other. The price point can also be a factor; wool felt is typically less expensive.

● **TIP** *What About People Who Are Allergic to Wool?*
As antithetical as that question might seem in a book about wool appliqué, allergy concerns are a reality for many people. Wool is a natural fiber that comes from, well, animals. Sheep to be more precise. While wool allergies are rare, sensitivities to wool are much more common and are believed to stem from the relative coarseness of the fibers in wool and how it feels on our skin. Different varieties of wool can have different coarseness levels, for example a soft Merino wool sweater versus a scratchy wool tartan blanket.

If you are allergic to wool or are making something for someone who is, an option to consider is felt made from a blend of bamboo. National Nonwovens has a line of bamboo/rayon felt blend that can be a good substitute for wool. Their line is called XoticFelt and comes in a range of colors. I have found it to be a bit softer than wool felt; I used it in my Love pillows (page 70).

Unwashed and washed felted wool squares and wool felt squares

Visual appearance between washed and un-washed felted wool and wool felt can be very different. The shrinkage rates can also be very noticeable.

In considering the examples above, you can see that washed and unwashed wool felt can have a very different texture and appearance. It's a matter of knowing what look you want in your finished project, what you are working with, and what it will do.

Like all fabric choices, ultimately it is up to you, and experimentation and personal choice are yours for the making. The projects in *Modern Wool* use both felted wool and wool felt, and those choices are noted in the individual project information so you can see the options yourself. Both types of wool can be used interchangeably in all the projects.

Textured (Patterned) Wool

Felted wool, unlike wool felt, can be found in a variety of print textures. Traditionally, these are plaids and other mottled patterns. These textures are also simply personal preference. Printed textures can add another layer of depth, interest, and detail to your appliqué, and they also tend to lend themselves to a softer visual effect when compared to crisper, sometimes more modern-leaning solids. But they shouldn't be ruled out! They can still find their place in modern projects. See Run (page 50) and Chill (page 32) for examples of incorporating textured wool into your projects.

Mixing Cotton and Wool

Traditional wool appliqué is often stitched on equally weighted solid wool background fabrics. But that doesn't mean wool appliqué can't be paired with cotton fabrics as well. Combining wool appliqué on cotton backgrounds creates an interesting contrast of textures and opens up a wide range of options for incorporating more modern fabrics in a typically traditional medium. Mixing cotton and wool is a bit more unexpected and the possibilities are endless.

Since my very first quilt project, I have always leaned toward a scrappy aesthetic, and being able to bring that scrappiness together with wool appliqué is a whole new world of design opportunity. In the process of trying to select background fabrics, I became enchanted with the difference a light or dark background can have on the exact same piece. I would lay out my appliqué pieces on a dark background and then a light and try to choose, which often proved impossible for me. Making each project in two different versions seemed to be my perfect solution!

Scrappy cotton backgrounds create an interesting counterpoint to wool appliqué. I think the saturated color of wool appliqué pieces is the perfect match to subtly blended scrappy backgrounds, both low-volume and darker print fabrics. Let's consider the mix of fabrics themselves.

LOW-VOLUME FABRICS

Low volume is a term familiar to most modern quilters and typically refers to fabrics that have a printed motif on a light background. Light is not limited to white. Traditionally we would look to white-on-white fabrics, but low volume encompasses so much more. The mixing of the printed fabrics and the subtle differences between them are what make them interesting to look at, in contrast to the brightly colored fabrics we love that often steal the show in our quilt projects.

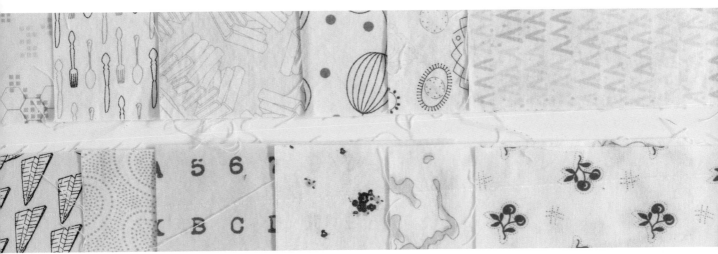

Examples of low-volume fabrics

When auditioning low-volume prints to include in your background mix, consider prints with pops of color or bolder designs. This may seem the opposite of what you want to do. Our eyes are built to detect differences in our environment and will always gravitate to the one print that stands out. But many of your pieces will be cut smaller and so you will see a limited amount of fabric. Also, as soon as the appliqué shapes are added, your eye will automatically be drawn away to them, making the backgrounds fade from attention. Keeping this in mind expands your options for mixing up the background fabrics enough to keep them interesting without having them take over the design.

Low-volume prints and low-volume prints with appliqué shapes added

THE DARK SIDE

You can achieve the same scrappy background in the opposite way by using dark background prints as well. The same concepts apply; use a variety of scales and prints and unify with a range of background colors instead of limiting to just one (such as varying shades or tones of black, dark gray, and so on) to create subtle interest in the backgrounds. It's important to include a variety of prints and pops of color that would surprise you—otherwise, if they are all just tonal in nature, the background will read as solid black.

Examples of dark prints

It's All Relative: A Little Color Theory and Trick of the Eye

Our eyeballs are amazing things! How we see and perceive color is fascinating and complex. Our eyes consist of cones and rods that perceive and register color, transmitting that information to our brains which leads to our determination of what "color" something is—or isn't.

Colors reside in a spectrum from ultraviolet to pale yellow. You may have heard of colors on the spectrum referred to in terms of temperature—*warm colors* (such as red, orange, and yellow) and *cool colors* (such as blue, green, and violet). Because our human eyes contain about two-thirds more cones than rods that sense these so-called warm colors, we are sensitive to more colors on the warm end of the color spectrum. But that doesn't mean there are less on the cool side, just that we have less of an ability to sense the differences between them.

Visible Spectrum

Red   Orange   Yellow   Green   Blue   Indigo   Violet

Warm Colors   **Cool Colors**

Seeing or perceiving color is not limited to the physical properties of our eyes. The color of an object often has less to do with the object itself and more to do with the effect of other colors around it and how they affect our perception because color is also relative. The X's in the images below appear to be two different colors because of their surroundings, but they are actually the same color (see the work of Josef Albers in Resources/Bibliography, page 126).

Thinking of colors in terms of temperature has also led to the idea that cool colors recede and warm colors advance. But temperature isn't the only thing that causes colors to recede or advance. It's also about what colors are around them or close by. And that leads us to black and white and what they do as backgrounds to our appliqué.

In light rays coming through a prism, white is really the coming together of all colors. Because they are made up of all the colors in the spectrum, white backgrounds have the highest level of competition in terms of reflecting all the colors. They can make colors placed on them appear to recede or fade and appear lighter in hue.

Black, on the other hand, is the absence of any color rays on the light spectrum. A black background doesn't compete with the colors in the same way and can actually make neighboring colors appear to advance or seem brighter in intensity. Another example inspired by the work of Josef Albers demonstrates this effect below. The red in both images is the same; it just appears lighter or darker in relation to the black or white sashing that surrounds it.

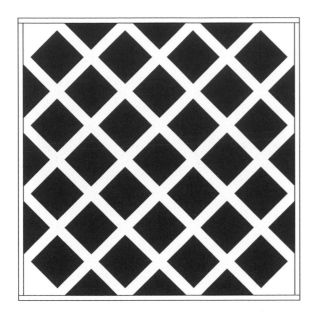 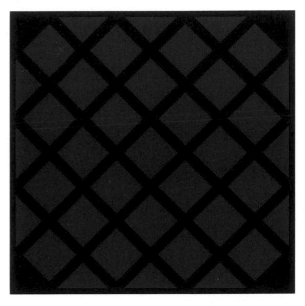

And we can't forget about our good friend *contrast*. Contrast is critical in geometric patterns because it is the variations of light and dark in the colors and how the pattern advances as our eyes follow across a traditional geometric quilt design.

Higher contrast allows for greater clarity of shapes, especially with cooler colors. In Chill (page 32), the cool purple and blue wool pennies stand out more clearly on the low-volume background. There is high contrast between the pennies and the white background. The dark version tends to blend the pennies into the black background because there is much less contrast with the cool purples and blues. Our eyes have more difficulty discerning where the pennies end and the background begins, suggesting the colors are receding.

The opposite is true with the warm appliqué colors in Rise (page 38). The warm oranges and reds are well defined against the dark backgrounds and thus seem to move forward. The same warm colors on the low-volume background are competing harder with the white which causes them to look lighter and recede.

And so it is with our *Modern Wool* projects. The colored appliqué shapes are exactly the same whether they are on the dark or low-volume backgrounds. It's only their relation to their backgrounds and the effects of the colors on each other which change our perception of them.

The real science and beauty are in deciding which version appeals to you.

TOOLS AND SUPPLIES

Thread

Thread options for wool appliqué are almost limitless. Personal preference, performance, and visual effect are the determining factors to consider. Size numbers associated with thread run in opposite directions. As the thread size number gets smaller, the thread size or thickness gets larger. For example, a 50-weight thread you would commonly use in your domestic machine for piecing will be much thinner than a 12-weight thread that you can use both for hand stitching and for machine appliqué.

Thread weights can have very different visual effects. An 8-weight perle cotton (also called pearl cotton) has a slightly chunkier, bolder appearance than a 12-weight perle cotton of the same color. Perle cotton threads are nondivisible, comprised of S-twisted threads, unlike six-strand embroidery threads that are separated to use and are untwisted. Because of these properties, perle cotton threads tend to lay on top of wool instead of sinking down into the wool like finer embroidery threads; they will be more visible (see Run, page 50).

Thread color and sheen will also affect the appearance of your projects. To have stitches that blend, choose colors that closely match your appliqué shapes (see Nosh, page 60) or that offer slight contrast. Choose colors in the same color family as your fabrics, that are complimentary to your design (see Rise, page 38, or Run, page 50).

To enhance the appearance of your stitches or make them stand out, choose strongly contrasting threads. For this look, I often like to use a basic white or black thread that corresponds to the scrappy backgrounds I have chosen (see Love, page 70, Gather, page 54, and Thrive, page 116) instead of matching my thread to the appliqué shape itself. The simplicity of the stitches stands out on the solid, saturated colors of the wool appliqué.

Wool threads will typically have a more matte finish, whereas cotton, synthetic, blended, and treated threads can have a glossier finish. Variegated threads are another option that can add dimension and texture to your stitches if that is your preference.

The differences can be subtle, and as with colors themselves, the choice is really yours. Like wool selections, I've noted the thread choices used in the various projects so you can see examples of some of the size and selection differences.

Thread Color Cocktail Party

One of the ways I like to think about selecting thread colors is to keep in mind what they are going to do or not do in my project. An analogy would be different guests at a cocktail party. There will be wallflowers, those that want to blend in and not draw attention to themselves at all. There will be minglers, those that will be uniquely themselves but will circulate and mix with others. And there will be those that want to stand out and be the life of the party—they are there to be noticed!

Thread can match exactly or very closely to the appliqué shapes and blend in very well. Matching thread color is a hallmark of traditional wool appliqué and is always a popular choice. This can also be of great benefit for novice stitchers that don't want their stitches to stand out; this can diminish the appearance of imperfections (see Nosh, page 60).

Minglers can be selected from the same related color family but not an exact match to the wool appliqué shapes. These are often analogous colors on the color wheel. They are designed to create interest and enhance a project without taking over (see Rise, page 38).

Then there are the standouts. These are the boldest of color choices. They can be complementary opposites on the color wheel (see Dwell, page 106) or black or white to match the background, not the appliqué shape (see Gather, page 54). You don't have to have perfect needlework to use a standout color thread. Just embrace the nature of hand stitching and its imperfections.

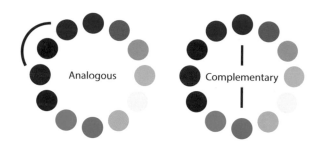

Analogous · Complementary

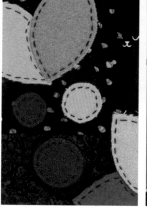
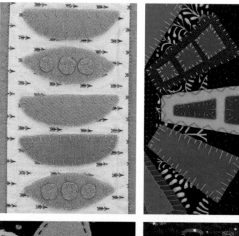
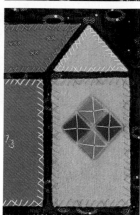

Close-ups of Nosh, Rise, Gather, and Dwell

Needles

For hand stitching, your choice of needle is partially determined by the type and size of thread you are stitching with. For wool appliqué, typical sizes that I use and prefer are chenille needles, size 22 or 24. Chenille needles have a large eye for easier threading with thicker threads and go easily through wool.

Thimbles are an option if you like them or if you find them helpful pushing through multiple layers. Often with wool appliqué, the needle goes through smoothly and you will find you won't always need a thimble.

Like thread choices, there are many needle sizes and options; it's really about experimenting and finding out what you prefer and what works for you.

Scissors

The best scissors I find for cutting wool are often simply the sharpest ones. A dull pair of scissors is not effective to make clean cuts in wool. I prefer medium 5″–6″ scissors instead of full-size 8″ scissors unless I'm cutting large shapes. Scissors with a smooth or serrated blade can be used. I also like to use my small 3″ pointed embroidery scissors for snipping in tighter areas and making small cuts.

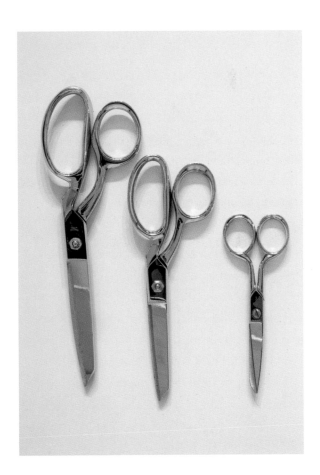

When cutting wool, try to keep your scissors at a right angle, or perpendicular, to the fabric instead of at a slanted angle and keep the fabric in the middle of the blades. I like to hold my scissors halfway open and move my wool piece under the blades as I cut. Some of the *Modern Wool* projects have wool shapes with straight edges and I like using my rotary cutter on those for a nice clean edge when I can.

WASHING AND CARE OF WOOL

The decision to prewash your fabrics, whether cotton or wool, is best made before you begin. I prefer to prewash all my cotton fabrics and selectively prewash my wool if necessary. If you are repurposing wool from old clothing, you will always want to prewash before using (see Repurposing Wool from Old Clothing, page 8).

All fabrics have some amount of shrinkage after being washed and they can shrink at different rates based on their weave, material, and quality among other things. Prewashing your cotton fabrics will remove finishing chemicals, such as sizing, that were used in the production and printing of the fabrics during the manufacturing process.

Some fabrics also have the potential to bleed and transfer their dyes to other neighboring fabrics (see *Tip:* Testing for Color Bleeding, page 9). This is particularly possible with hand-dyed wool fabrics that may not be color safe. I would rather these possibilities be dealt with before they get into my project where I can't control them or their effects as easily. Prewashing levels the playing field of your fabrics before you put them into a project.

While I like to prewash my cotton fabrics, I prefer to *not* prewash my wool unless I need to for colorfastness. I like the more finished look of commercially prepared pre-felted wool and wool felt. Hand dyed wool cuts have already been washed and felted during the dyeing process. Of course, like everything else, this is a matter of preference. With some fabrics, it won't make much difference at all. Sometimes the differences can be more dramatic.

I generally suggest that you don't wash your wool projects after completion, but sometimes life has other ideas and you need to. It's not that wool can't be washed, it absolutely can. It's just that like any quilt, the appearance will change, especially when factoring in shrinkage in the batting and so on.

Completed projects can be shaken for dust or spot cleaned as needed. A lint roller or damp cloth can take care of minor things. They can also be dry-cleaned. Just keep in mind that the process of felting wool uses water, heat, and agitation to felt the wool. Continuing to do that will give you more of what you already have, so to keep your projects as crisp and defined as they can be, keep washing to a minimum. Of course, some of the *Modern Wool* projects are only suitable for surface cleaning, such as the Run clock (page 50) and the Push pincushion (page 86).

Sample felted wool appliqué leaf blocks, quilted with batting and backing, before and after washing

METHODS

Appliqué Basics

Appliqué pieces can be prepared and temporarily held in place for stitching in a variety of ways. Common techniques include using appliqué pins, appliqué glue, basting stitches, and fusible web.

FREEZER-PAPER METHOD

One traditional way to prepare your pieces is using the freezer-paper technique. Freezer paper comes on a roll and can be found in your local grocery store. It is also available in packages of precut 8½″ × 11″ sheets (such as Quilter's Freezer Paper Sheets by C&T Publishing). It has a dull paper side that you trace your image on and a shiny, waxy side that is fused temporarily onto your fabric with an iron. For wool appliqué, you can choose to fuse the freezer paper onto either side of the piece of wool since both sides are the same. You would then use pins, dots of appliqué glue, or basting stitches to secure the shapes to the background for stitching.

FUSIBLE APPLIQUÉ

For all the projects in this book, I've chosen to use fusible web to create and attach the appliqué shapes to the background fabric prior to stitching. Once the pieces are fused in place, they are very mobile-friendly and can easily be taken on the go. There is no worry of dealing with pins (being poked with pins in my case!) or losing pieces.

Fusible web also lends stability to the appliqué pieces on cotton backgrounds. Wool appliqué is traditionally done on an equally weighted wool background. Since we don't have that by using cotton backgrounds instead, the fusible will add stability to the wool appliqué pieces so they will remain smooth without puckering or distorting.

Also, one of the best benefits of fusible web is the stability it lends to the raw cut edge of some loosely woven wool fabrics. Although naturally much less so than cotton fabric, like any other woven fabric, the edges of wool can fray if not turned under or stabilized. In effect, some stitches, such as the blanket stitch, are designed to finish the edge to prevent fraying. But there are a variety of other stitches that I like to use, such as a simple running stitch, that don't provide that stability. This is where fusible web comes in handy, allowing for a raw edge with no need for stitches to hold it secure.

For wool appliqué, my preference is to use SoftFuse Premium Paperbacked Fusible Web (by Sulky), a paper-backed fusible web for machine or hand appliqué. It is very lightweight, adheres well to both wool and cotton, and is hardly noticeable while you are hand stitching through it, making it a great option.

● TIP *Fusing in Place*
It is much easier to position wool appliqué elements on backgrounds using a pressing surface as a work surface instead of trying to move the piece from another location to the pressing surface and have things slip and slide out of place.

USING PATTERNS

Any time you are using fusible web for appliqué, the patterns are drawn in reverse because you attach the fusible to the wrong side of the fabric. When the appliqué shape is fused to the background, the pattern or shape is oriented in the right direction. For that reason, all the patterns in these projects are drawn in reverse, although in many cases (such as with circles, leaves, and so on) there isn't any difference in direction.

Often with wool fabrics and always with wool felt, the right and wrong sides are exactly the same or very close, so you can fuse your patterns to either side without much worry. I have noticed on some wool pieces one side appears a bit fuzzier than the other and there can be color variations, especially in hand-dyed pieces. It is up to you and your personal preference which you choose to use.

NOTE If you opt to use the freezer-paper method, you don't need to be concerned with the reverse image in that you can attach the freezer paper on either side of your wool. The freezer paper will be peeled off when placing on your background and you can flip your appliqué shape in either direction. If you choose to do the appliqué in cotton or some other single sided print fabric, you'll need to keep the reverse image idea in mind.

The first step is to trace the pattern onto the paper side of the fusible web product. Some have only one side of paper backing, some have two. Refer to the manufacturer's instructions for whichever product you are using. Lay the fusible over the pattern and trace directly on the pattern lines using a nonsmudging pencil.

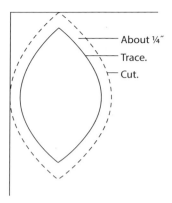

About ¼"
Trace.
Cut.

Cut outside the traced shape, leaving approximately ¼" extra space around the traced shape.

Place the traced shape on your wool and fuse together using the cotton setting on your iron. Refer to the manufacturer's instructions for the product you are using for best heat and steam settings.

Cut out the appliqué shape, cutting directly on the traced line of the pattern. Remove the backing paper, position on your background fabric, and fuse into place with the iron. I like to turn the steam back on at this point and give it a shot of steam from the back side of the background fabric to secure the appliqué pieces into place. Be sure to refer to the manufacturer's instructions for any product. Using an iron that is too hot or leaving the iron in place for too long can actually burn away the adhesive properties of the fusible.

● **TIP** *Saving Space, Less Waste*
When preparing multiple shapes in the same color of wool, you can trace your shapes tightly together without any spacing in between. After the fusible is attached to the wool, you will be cutting directly on the drawn lines since you won't need to have any additional space for a seam allowance.

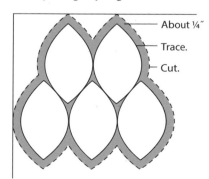

About ¼"
Trace.
Cut.

Stitches

Common embroidery stitches are used in these projects to attach and embellish the wool appliqué shapes. Refer to the project photos if you want to copy my stitch choices, or branch out on your own and switch things up!

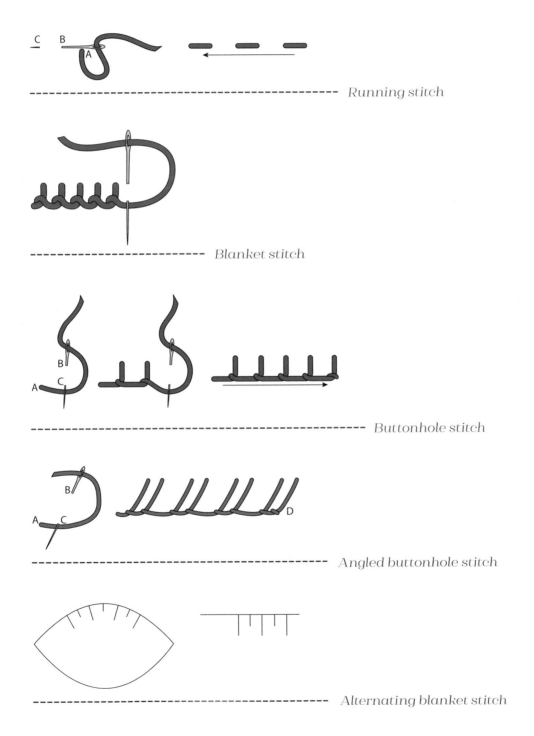

Running stitch

Blanket stitch

Buttonhole stitch

Angled buttonhole stitch

Alternating blanket stitch

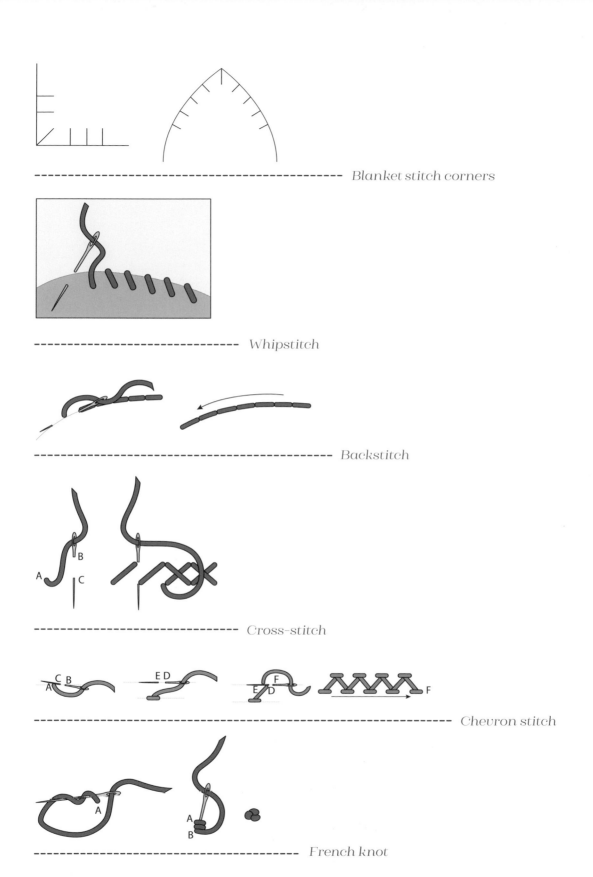

-- Blanket stitch corners

---------------------------- Whipstitch

-- Backstitch

---------------------------- Cross-stitch

-- Chevron stitch

---------------------------------- French knot

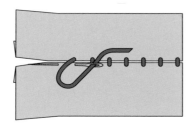

Lazy daisy stitch

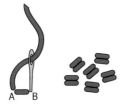

------------------- *Seed stitch*

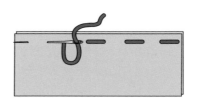

--------------------------- *Slip stitch*   --------------------------- *Basting stitch*

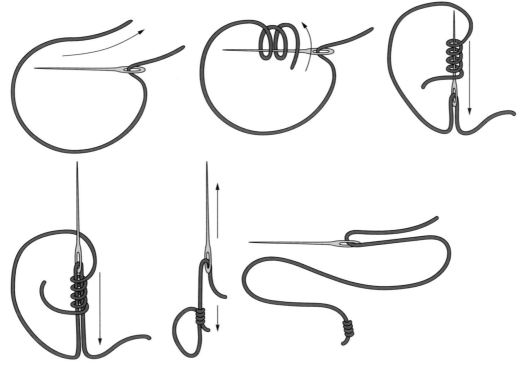

-- *Quilter's knot at end of thread*

Basic Binding Instructions

The yardage calculations and cutting directions for each of the projects that follow specify the number of strips you'll need—all cut 2¼″–wide across the width of the fabric (WOF). I generally prefer 2¼″–wide strips for these smaller scale projects, but you may cut narrower or wider strips if you prefer.

Preparing Bias-Cut Binding

Cutting fabric strips for binding on the bias of the fabric creates more flexibility for binding curved edges, such as circles and rounded corners in some of these projects. The binding process is the same except for how you make the initial strip cuts. There are different ways to do this but for our smaller projects, this straight-forward technique is a good choice.

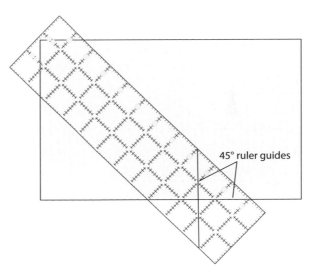

45° ruler guides

1. Start with a square or rectangle of fabric opened flat as a single layer. Align the 45° line of a long rotary-cutting ruler with the straightened or selvage edge nearest you. Cut along the right edge of the ruler.

2. To make the first strip, align the 2¼″ line on your ruler with the angled edge of the fabric.

Cut along the right side of the ruler again. Continue until you have the number of strips required to total the length for your project.

3. Sew the strips together to complete the length you need. Continue with Basic Binding Instructions, Step 2.

1. Cut the binding strips and sew them together, using diagonal seams. Trim, leaving a ¼" seam allowance, and press the seam allowances open. *figs A–C*

2. Fold the binding strip in half lengthwise, wrong sides together. Press the entire length of the binding. *fig D*

3. On the front of quilt, begin in the middle of one side. Align the raw edges of the binding with the raw edge of the quilt. Leave a tail about 6" from the start of the binding and sew, using ¼" seam allowance and a walking foot. Stop stitching ¼" from the first corner and backstitch a couple of stitches to secure. Cut the threads and remove the quilt from under the presser foot. *fig E*

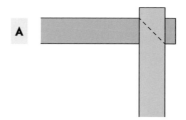

A

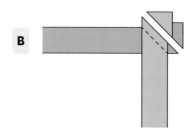

B

C

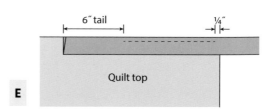

D   Foldline

6" tail   ¼"

Quilt top

E

4. Turn the quilt so you're ready to sew the next side. Flip the binding strip up and away from the quilt at a 90° angle, and then fold it back down on itself so that the fold is even with the edge of the quilt. *figs F–G*

5. Start stitching at the fold, again taking a couple of backstitches to secure the stitching and continue stitching down the second side until you are ¼″ from the next corner. Stop, backstitch, cut the thread, and fold the binding as before. Continue around the quilt, stopping about 8″ from your starting point on the first side. Cut the thread and remove the quilt from the machine.

6. Overlap the end of the binding and the beginning of the binding tail. Trim the ends with a perpendicular cut so that there is a 2¼″ overlap. The overlap distance should be equal to the cut width of your binding strip. *fig H*

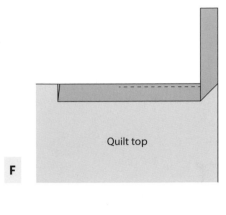

F

Quilt top

G

Quilt top

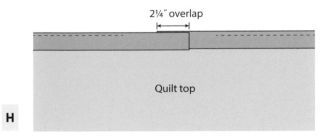

2¼″ overlap

H

Quilt top

7. Open up the 2 ends of the binding and place the tails right sides together at a right angle as shown. Mark a diagonal line from corner to corner and pin the ends together. *fig I*

8. Stitch the binding ends together along the marked line. Trim the seam allowances to ¼″ and finger-press the seam allowances open. Refold the binding and align the raw edges with the quilt top. Finish sewing the binding to the quilt. *figs J–K*

9. Flip the binding out and press it toward the outside edge. Turn the binding to the back of the quilt and stitch by hand using a whipstitch. *fig L*

⬤ TIP *Binding Completely by Machine*
To add binding completely by machine, repeat Basic Binding Instructions, Steps 1–9 (pages 28–30); *except*, in Step 3, start by attaching the prepared binding strip to the back of the quilt in the middle of one side. Continue as instructed. When you get to Step 9, turn the binding to the front of the quilt sandwich and stitch to secure with either a straight stitch or decorative stitch on your machine instead of by hand.

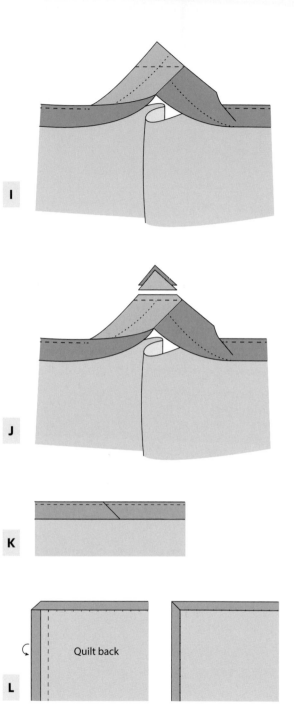

I

J

K

L

Quilt back

PROJECTS

Each of the twelve *Modern Wool* projects are shown in both low-volume and dark printed fabric background variations. The fabric and supply amounts listed in the project instructions are to make one project version unless otherwise noted.

While one of my main design components of the projects is using the scrappy backgrounds, that is not always what everyone needs or wants to do. With that in mind, I've included alternate single-fabric background options listed for each project with the measurement of the background for easy substitution of a single fabric, if you so choose.

Project instructions include numbered and lettered patterns and layout images to help with appliqué placement but should be considered suggestions and not necessarily rules. Feel free to experiment and change up the layouts to make your project unique and your own.

The same applies to the stitches you choose to use on your projects. I've endeavored to show you a variety of stitches, thread choices, and design options, but ultimately the projects are yours and you should always feel empowered to make your own design decisions for what you find pleasing and enjoyable to do. Use my examples as a starting point for your own creativity.

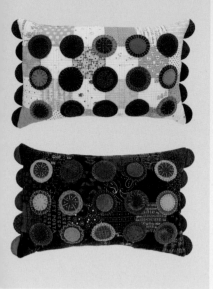

CHILL

FINISHED CUSHION: 18″ × 12″

It's time to relax! Chill is inspired by traditional wool penny rugs. Small scraps of wool were saved and cut into circles or "pennies" and were typically stitched onto a wool background or even connected edge to edge with simple or fancy stitches to make table mats or actual rugs. With that inspiration, the modern pennies in Chill find a new home on this cozy throw cushion to brighten up any seating area.

Materials

If you want your project to be entirely scrappy without repeating prints, use the highest number of suggested prints in the range and make sure all pieces are at least the minimum size.

Low-volume or dark prints: 18–24 assorted scraps, minimum 3½″ × 3½″ square.
Or use alternate single-fabric background option: ⅜ yard.

Striped print: ⅜ yard for cushion back

Wool: 8–12 selections (6½″ × 8″ each) in a variety of magentas, teals, blues, and purples for pennies

Scrap fabric or muslin: 17″ × 23″ for back of quilted cushion front (This will be inside the cushion and will not be visible in the finished project.)

Batting: 17″ × 23″

Pillow form: 18″ × 12″

Project Particulars

For my project as shown, I used wool scraps, some solids, and some that included small checks and patterns. The stitching on this project is really a sampler of many of the stitches featured throughout the book (see Stitches, page 24). I used a variety of threads in coordinating colors including 8- and 10-weight perle cotton, as well as 12-weight cotton thread.

Cutting

Low-volume or dark prints

- Cut 24 squares 3½″ × 3½″.
  Or use alternate single-fabric background option:
  1 rectangle 12½″ × 18½″.

Striped print

- Cut 1 rectangle 12½″ × 18½″.

Construction

Seam allowances for piecing and construction are ¼" throughout.

PIECE THE BACKGROUND

If using the alternate single-fabric background, skip to Prepare the Appliqué Pieces (below).

1. Arrange the 3½" squares in 4 rows of 6 squares each.

2. Sew the squares into rows. Press the seams in each row in alternating directions.

3. Sew the rows together. Press the final seams between rows in any direction you prefer. *fig A*

PREPARE THE APPLIQUÉ PIECES

1. Follow the general directions in Appliqué Basics (page 22) to prepare your appliqué pieces.

2. Prepare the number of pieces indicated on the patterns (see Chill Patterns, page 36).

3. If you are using the single-fabric option, divide the large rectangle into 24 "blocks" by using a chalk pencil or water-soluble marker and making 5 marks first at 3¼" from the left edge and at 3" intervals horizontally across the 18½" width; repeat vertically down the 12½" height making 3 marks, the first 3¼" down from the top. Use the intersections of the marks to help with appliqué placement.

PROJECT ASSEMBLY

1. Place the wool appliqué pieces on the pieced background. The large wool pennies are centered over the seam intersections of the background squares. Use the diagram for placement. Stack a smaller penny on each larger one. *fig B*

2. When you are satisfied with the placement, fuse the wool pieces to the backgrounds.

3. Hand stitch the wool pennies as desired.

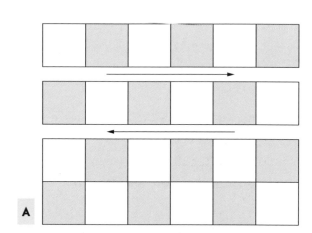

A

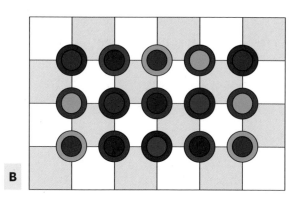

B

> ### *Quilting Idea*
> I chose to quilt my project using a matchstick plaid design on my domestic machine. This stitch is done with the walking foot and is easy to plan and execute.

FINISHING

1. Layer and quilt as desired. *fig C*

2. Trim the quilted cushion front to 12½″ × 18½″.

3. To prepare the wool pennies for the side trim, make 5 pairs of blue and purple pennies from the remaining pattern A circles. Fuse together and whipstitch (see Stitches, page 24) all the way around each pair. Press to set the stitches.

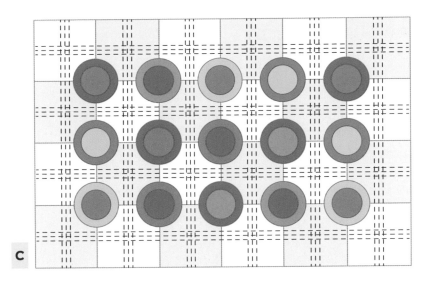

C

4. Cut the joined pairs in half. Handle these halves gently and infrequently. There are loose threads that will separate easily until they are secured in the sides of the cushion. *fig D*

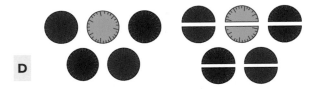

D

5. Select 5 half-circles from Step 4. With the cushion front right side facing up on your work surface, place the half-circles along each short end side by side in an arrangement of your liking. Align the flat edge of each half-circle along the edge of the cushion front. Leave ½″ space from each corner uncovered. *fig E*

6. When you are satisfied with their arrangement, pin each half-circle to the cushion front to hold in place while continuing with the next steps.

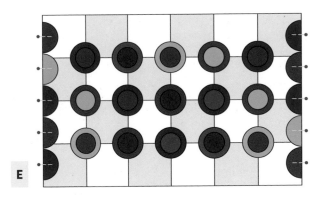

E

7. Lay the cushion back fabric 12½″ × 18½″ rectangle on top, right sides together. All the half-circles should be hidden from view. Add pins all the way along the outer edge.

8. Use the walking foot on your machine and a ¼″ seam allowance to stitch down the short ends first to secure all the fringe half-pennies. Go slowly, removing pins from the pennies as you approach them, adjusting pennies if necessary. This will seem thick but will be fine if you go slowly. Stitch down the full length of the short sides.

9. Next, stitch down the long sides, leaving an 8″ opening unsewn on the bottom edge. *fig F*

10. Snip the points of each corner to remove bulk, being careful not to cut into stitching. *fig G*

11. Turn the cushion cover inside out. Push out the seams and corners with your finger or a dull turning tool. Fold the seam allowances at the opening to the inside. Press the cushion cover from the back with an iron to set the seams and the folds at the opening solidly. *fig H*

12. Insert the pillow form and close the opening with a small whipstitch or slip stitch (see Stitches, page 24) with matching thread.

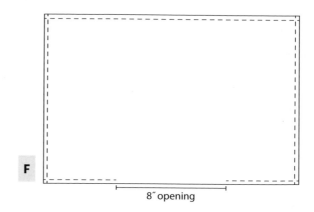

F

8″ opening

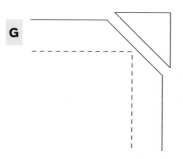

G

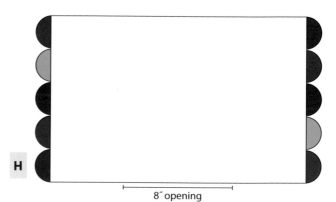

H

8″ opening

CHILL PATTERNS

Chill

B penny
Cut 15.

Chill

A penny
Cut 25.

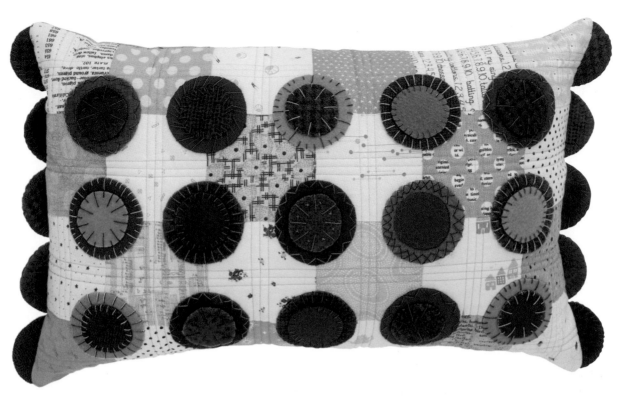

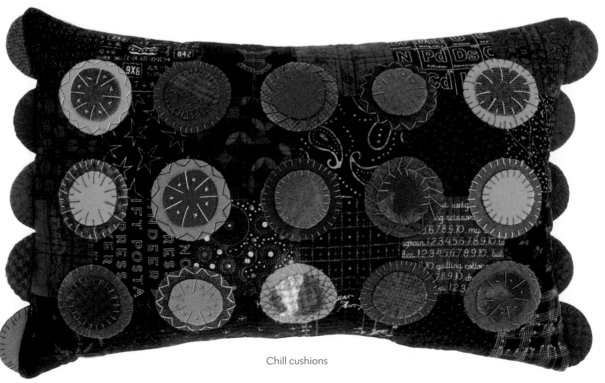

Chill cushions

RISE

FINISHED BLOCK: 12″ × 12″
FINISHED RUNNER: 12½″ × 36½″

The Rise table runner project features a deconstructed Dresden plate design. The straight-edge blades of each block create a simple yet effective place to feature a variety of stitches and threads for your tabletop. Pick your version for morning, evening, or anytime to match your decor.

Materials

If you want your project to be entirely scrappy without repeating prints, use the highest number of suggested prints in the range and make sure all pieces are at least the minimum size.

Low-volume or dark prints: 9–18 assorted 2½″ strips, minimum 12½″ length.
Or use alternate single-fabric background option: ⅜ yard.

Wool: 6–8 selections (6½″ × 8″ each) in a variety of warm tones such as orange, red, gold, salmon, and yellow

Binding fabric: ¼ yard

Backing fabric: ½ yard

Batting: 17″ × 41″

> ### *Project Particulars*
>
> For my project as shown, I used felted wool from Local Farm Girl (see Resources, page 126) in the 03 and 04 ranges of the following colors: Bright Red, Red Lichen, Sunflower, and Carrot. I used the following stitches: whipstitch, alternating blanket stitch, cross-stitch, and chevron stitch (see Stitches, page 24) and a variety of 12-weight cotton threads.

Cutting

Low-volume or dark prints

- Cut 18 strips 2½″ × 12½″.
  Or use alternate single-fabric background option:
  1 rectangle 12½″ × 36½″.

Binding

- Cut 3 strips 2¼″ × WOF.

Backing

- Cut 1 rectangle 17″ × 41″.

Construction

Seam allowances for piecing and construction are ¼″ throughout.

PIECE THE BLOCKS

If using the alternate single-fabric background, skip to Prepare the Appliqué Pieces (below).

1. Select 6 background strips and arrange in order of your liking.

2. Sew together along the long edges of the strips into a strip set block. Press the seams in any direction. *fig A*

3. Trim block to 12½″ × 12½″ if necessary. Repeat to make 3 background blocks.

PREPARE THE APPLIQUÉ PIECES

1. Follow the general directions in Appliqué Basics (page 22) to prepare your appliqué pieces.

2. Prepare the number of pieces indicated on the patterns (see Rise Patterns, page 43).

3. If you are using the single-fabric option, divide the large rectangle into 3 "blocks" by making 2 folds 12½″ in from each end. Use the fold lines to help with appliqué placement. Go to Block Assembly, Step 2 (next page) to continue.

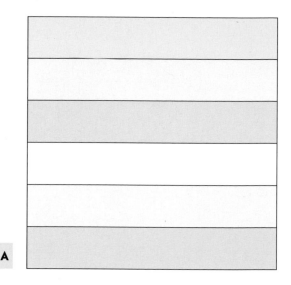

A

Cutting Tip

For faster and easier preparation of these straight-edge appliqué pieces, use a rotary cutter and an acrylic straight-edge ruler of any size instead of scissors to cut out your pieces.

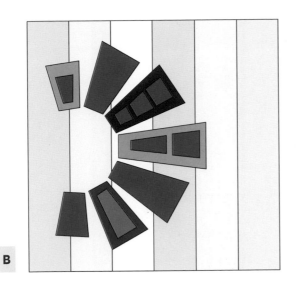

B

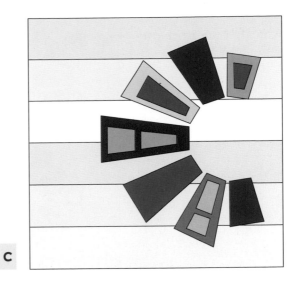

C

BLOCK ASSEMBLY

1. Place the wool appliqué pieces on each background block. I chose to alternate the direction of the background strips in each block. Two blocks are oriented vertically, and one is horizontal. *figs B–D*

2. For help with appliqué placement, use a 4″ circle (such as a coaster or a small saucer) at the base of each block to help arrange the wool pieces. Be sure to keep your pieces out of the seam allowance area. *fig E*

3. When you are satisfied with the placement, fuse the wool pieces to the backgrounds.

4. Hand stitch as desired.

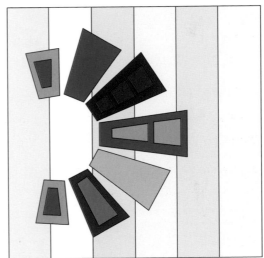

D

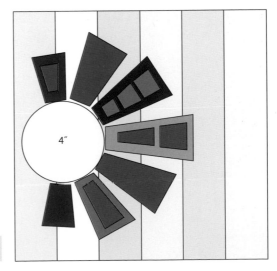

E

PROJECT ASSEMBLY

Sew the blocks into a row. The pieced top should measure 12½″ × 36½″. *fig F*

FINISHING

Layer, quilt, and bind as desired.

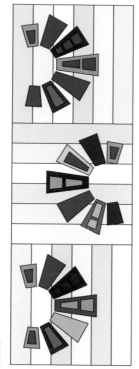

F

Block layout

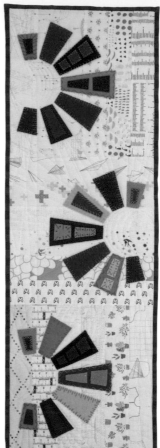

Rise table runners, quilting by Tracey Fisher

Quilting Idea

The quilting on this project was done on a longarm machine by Tracey Fisher. The same pattern can be achieved using the walking foot on your domestic machine.

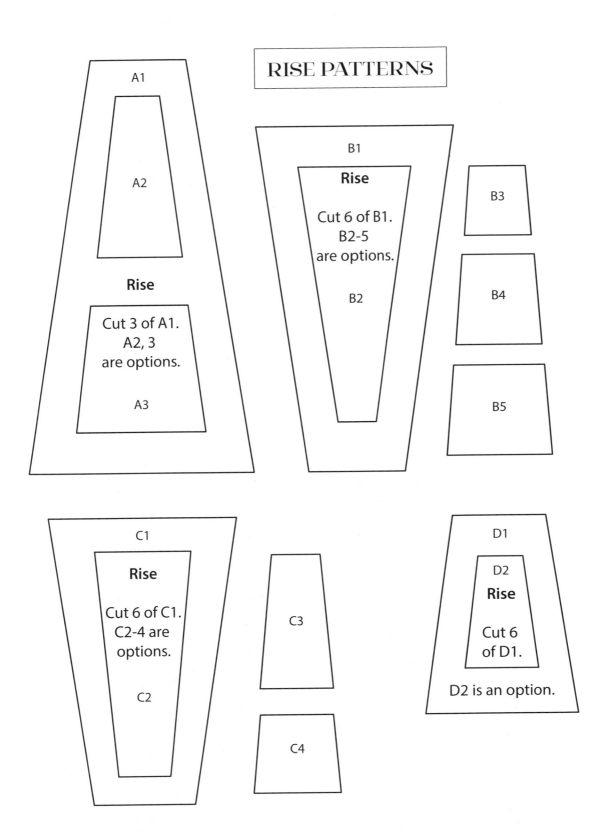

RISE PATTERNS

A1

A2

Rise

Cut 3 of A1.
A2, 3
are options.

A3

B1

Rise

Cut 6 of B1.
B2-5
are options.

B2

B3

B4

B5

C1

Rise

Cut 6 of C1.
C2-4 are
options.

C2

C3

C4

D1

D2

Rise

Cut 6
of D1.

D2 is an option.

REST

FINISHED MAT: 6″ circle

Two simple shapes and three different layout suggestions makes for a fast, fun, and functional project in Rest. Create a landing spot for your cuppa and also make some for friends. Like potato chips, you'll be hard-pressed to stop at just one.

Materials

If you want your project to be entirely scrappy without repeating prints, use the highest number of suggested prints in the range and make sure all pieces are at least the minimum size.

Amounts given are enough for 3 mats.

Low-volume or dark prints: 12–18 assorted 1½″ strips, minimum 8″ length.
Or use alternate single-fabric background option: 1 fat quarter.

Wool: 3 selections (6½″ × 8″ each) of teal, pink, and magenta

Binding fabric: ½ yard

Backing fabric: ¼ yard

Batting: 3 squares 7″ × 7″

Project Particulars

For my project as shown I used WoolFelt in pinks and teal from National Nonwovens (see Resources, page 126). For the appliqué, I used a running stitch (see Stitches, page 24) and 12-weight cotton thread.

Cutting

Low-volume or dark prints

- Cut 18 strips 1½″ × 8″.
  Or use alternate single-fabric background option:
  3 squares 7″ × 7″.

Binding

- Cut 3 bias strips 2¼″ × 25″.

Backing

- Cut 3 squares 7″ × 7″.

Construction

Seam allowances for piecing and construction are ¼″ throughout.

PIECE THE BACKGROUND BLOCKS

If using the alternate single-fabric background, skip to Step 3.

1. Select 6 background strips. Arrange in order of your liking.

2. Sew the long edges of the strips together into a strip set block. Press the seams in any direction. *fig A*

3. Trace a 6″ circle on the right side of each background block. This will be your guide for appliqué placement. Do *not* cut out the circle at this point.

A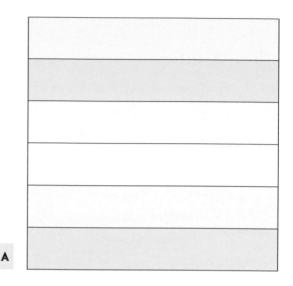

Rest mug mats

PREPARE THE APPLIQUÉ PIECES

Follow the general directions in Appliqué Basics (page 22) to prepare your appliqué pieces. Prepare the number of pieces indicated on the pattern page (see Rest Patterns, page 49).

PROJECT ASSEMBLY

1. Using the diagrams and the photos for reference, place the wool appliqué pieces on the background circles, being sure to stay at least ¼″ in from the drawn circle line. That will be the seam allowance for the binding. *figs B–D*

2. When you are satisfied with the placement, fuse the wool pieces to the backgrounds.

3. Hand stitch as desired.

FINISHING

1. Layer with backing and batting and quilt as desired.

2. Trim to 6″ circles.

3. Finish with binding cut on the bias so that it will curve smoothly around the circles (see Preparing Bias-Cut Binding, page 27).

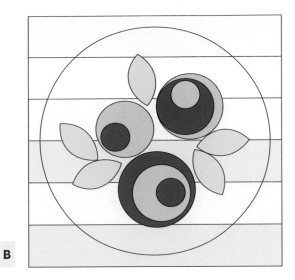

B

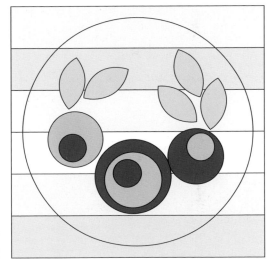

C

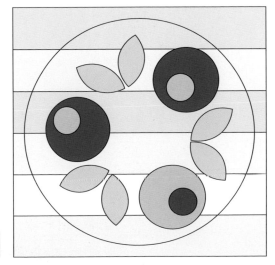

D

Binding on a Curve

1. Begin to attach the prepared bias binding strip to the front of your project just like you would with regular binding. Leave 3″–4″ for a tail. *fig A*

2. Stop and leave a space of about 3″ open. *fig B*

3. Trim one tail at an angle. Trim the other straight across the end. The two tails should overlap by about 2″. Fold the end of the straight-cut tail under to finish and press. *fig C*

4. Tuck the angle-cut tail into the folded-edge tail. Continue to sew the binding to attach. *fig D*

5. Fold the attached binding over to the back side of your project and clip or pin into place. Complete by hand stitching down with a small whipstitch. *fig E*

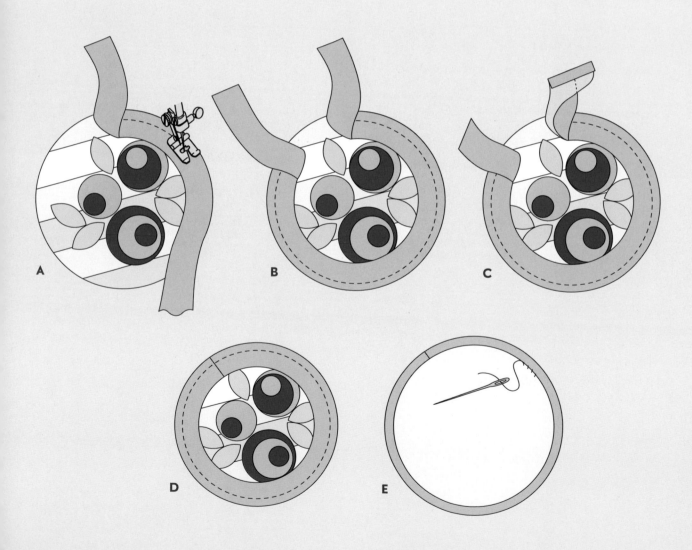

REST PATTERNS

	Pattern	Quantity
Layout 1	Circle A	1
	Circle B	1
	Circle C	3
	Circle D	3
	Leaf	5
Layout 2	Circle A	1
	Circle C	3
	Circle D	3
	Leaf	5
Layout 3	Circle C	3
	Circle D	3
	Leaf	6

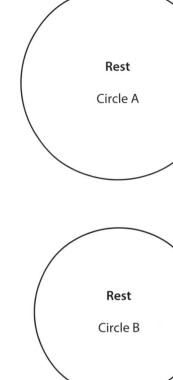

Rest

Circle A

Rest

Circle B

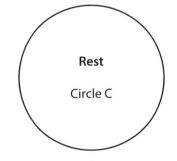

Rest

Circle C

Rest

Circle D

Rest

Leaf

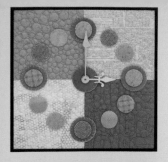

RUN

FINISHED CLOCKFACE: 12″ × 12″

Wool seems to fit in everywhere, even on the face of a clock! Wool pennies are the perfect size to define this clockface project, Run.

Materials

If you want your project to be entirely scrappy without repeating prints, use the highest number of suggested prints in the range and make sure all pieces are at least the minimum size.

Low-volume or dark prints: 2–4 fabrics, minimum 8″ × 8″ square.
Or use alternate single-fabric background option: 1 fat quarter.

Wool: 3–5 selections (6½″ × 4″ each) in green and 1 in teal (6½″ × 8″) for wool pennies

Muslin or scrap fabric: 18″ × 18″ for back of quilt sandwich
(will not show in finished project)

Batting: 18″ × 18″

Other supplies

Album cover frame: 12″ × 12″, board included

Clock mechanism with hands: Battery operated

Drill with bit: To make the hole for the clock mechanism (check packaging for bit size)

Adhesive spray

Duct tape

Cutting

Low-volume or dark prints

• Cut 4 squares 8″ × 8″.
 Or use alternate single-fabric background option:
 1 square 16″ × 16″. Then continue to Prepare the Appliqué Pieces (page 22).

> ### Project Particulars
> The extra items for this project, the album cover frame and clock mechanism, can commonly be found at chain craft stores or general goods stores. For my project as shown, I used a variety of wool from my scrap bin. For the stitching, I used a blanket stitch (see Stitches, page 24) in a coordinating 8-weight perle cotton.

Run clockfaces, quilting by Tracey Fisher

Construction

Seam allowances for piecing and construction are ¼" throughout.

PIECE THE BACKGROUND

Arrange the four 8" squares as you like. Join into a large four-patch block. Press the seams in any direction. *fig A*

PREPARE THE APPLIQUÉ PIECES

Follow the general directions in Appliqué Basics (page 22) to prepare your appliqué pieces. Prepare the number of pieces indicated on the patterns (see Run Patterns, page 53).

APPLIQUÉ AND QUILTING

1. Place a 6½" circle such as a salad plate in the center of the background square to help arrange the wool pennies around the clockface.

2. Arrange 4 large teal A pennies at the 12, 3, 6, and 9 positions first. Then place 8 smaller green B pennies on the remaining hours. *fig B*

3. Remove the plate or circle from the center. Place the remaining large teal A penny in the center. Stack the remaining 4 green B pennies on top of the large teal quarter hours. Fuse into place.

4. Hand stitch the appliqué as desired.

5. Layer the 18" × 18" muslin or scrap fabric square, batting, and appliquéd clockface. Baste and quilt as desired.

6. Trim to 16" × 16".

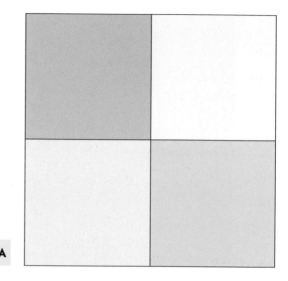

A

Fusing in Place

Arrange your wool pennies on your clockface while it's laying on your pressing surface. With so many small pieces, it's easy for things to shift and slide in transit to your pressing surface.

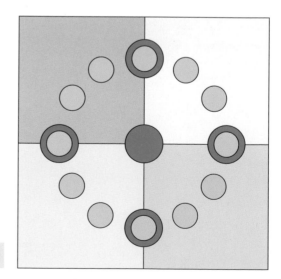

B

PROJECT ASSEMBLY

1. Remove the backboard from the album frame. On one side, draw diagonal lines in both directions, corner to corner, to locate and mark the center of the board.

2. Drill a hole—just large enough to fit the clock mechanism—directly in the center of the board. Refer to clock mechanism instructions for the exact bit size required. *fig C*

3. Center the quilted clockface on the board's front to confirm fit. Remove it and spray the board with the adhesive spray.

4. Replace the quilted clockface, making sure it's centered, and press to adhere. Smooth out any bumps or wrinkles until it is firmly secured.

5. Wrap the extra quilt edges around to the back of the board and secure with duct tape. *fig D*

6. With sharp pointed scissors, from the back, gently poke a hole in the center of the quilt face where it aligns with the center hole. Take a few small snips, just enough to fit the clock mechanism through.

7. Insert the clock mechanism and add the clock hands on the front following the manufacturer's instructions.

8. Mount in the frame and secure.

C

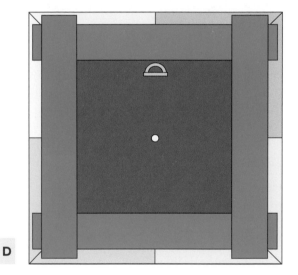

D

RUN PATTERNS

Run

B penny
Cut 12.

Run

A penny
Cut 5.

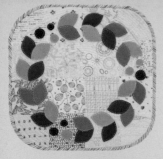

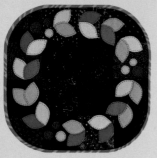

GATHER

FINISHED TABLE TOPPER: 18½″ × 18½″

A wreath of laurel leaves and berries creates a centerpiece focus in Gather. Gather is a fine example of two simple shapes, the leaf and the circle, coming together to create a pleasing and balanced design. Whether destined to be a resting place for your favorite candle or vase, or to simply stand alone, Gather will greet everyone at your table.

Materials

If you want your project to be entirely scrappy without repeating prints, use the highest number of suggested prints in the range and make sure all pieces are at least the minimum size.

Low-volume or dark prints: 10–16 assorted fabrics, minimum 5″ × 5″ square.
Or use alternate single-fabric background option: ⅝ yard.

Wool: 6–8 selections (6½″ × 4″ each) in a variety of greens for leaves

Wool scraps: Minimum 3″ × 3″ squares in pink and magenta for berries

Binding fabric: ¼ yard

Backing fabric: ½ yard

Batting: 23″ × 23″

> ### Project Particulars
>
> For my project as shown, I used felted wool from Andover Fabrics in the following colors: WoolWerks Fresh for the leaves and WoolWerks Fire for the berries. The 5″ charm square pack is a great option for this project. You can get 4 leaves out of each square of wool leaving a few extras and lots of options. For the stitching, I used a simple running stitch (see Stitches, page 24) in either black or white 12-weight cotton thread.

Cutting

Low-volume or dark prints

- Cut 16 squares 5″ × 5″.
  Or use alternate single-fabric background option:
  1 square 18½″ × 18½″.

Binding

- Cut 4 bias binding strips 2¼″ × 25″.

Backing

- Cut 1 square 23″ × 23″.

Construction

Seam allowances for piecing and construction are ¼″ throughout.

PIECE THE BACKGROUND

If using the alternate single-fabric background, skip to Prepare the Appliqué Pieces (below).

1. Arrange the 5″ squares in 4 rows of 4 squares each.

2. Sew the squares into rows. Press the seams in each row in alternating directions.

3. Sew the rows together. Press the final seams between rows in any direction you prefer. *fig A*

4. Do *not* trim the rounded corners until instructed, after quilting.

PREPARE THE APPLIQUÉ PIECES

Follow the general directions in Appliqué Basics (page 22) to prepare your appliqué pieces. Prepare the number of pieces indicated on the patterns (see Gather Patterns, page 58).

PROJECT ASSEMBLY

1. Place the wool appliqué pieces on the pieced background. *fig B*

2. For help with appliqué placement, use a 9″ circle (such as a dinner plate) in the center of the pieced background. This will help with arranging the leaves and berries.

3. When you are satisfied with the placement, fuse the wool pieces to the background.

4. Hand stitch as desired.

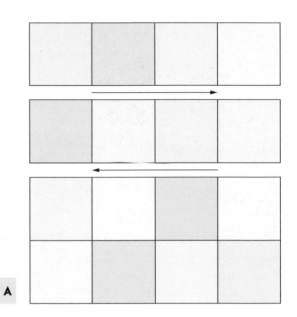

A

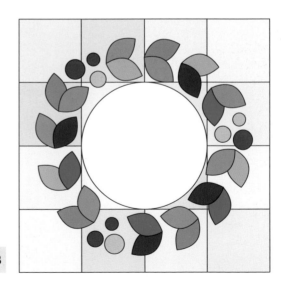

B

FINISHING

1. Layer and quilt as desired.

Spiral Quilting with the Walking Foot

The quilting motif I chose to do on this project was spiral quilting, using the walking foot on my domestic machine.

Spiral quilting is a continuous line motif. I start by marking the center of my project with a round C to begin my quilting. A quarter is a perfect sized template to use. You want your C to be perfectly round.

Begin stitching at the bottom of the C directly on the marked line. You will stitch in a clockwise direction which means you will be turning your quilt sandwich in a counterclockwise direction under the presser foot.

Go very slowly on the first rotation, a couple of stitches at a time, adjusting the piece under the presser foot until you come to the top of the C. Continue stitching, gradually angling off the marked line until the left side of your presser foot becomes aligned with the previous line of stitching. It will begin to look like this:

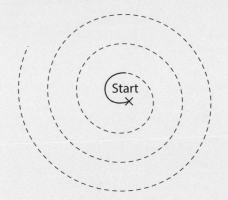

Continue the spiral stitching until you reach the end of the inside circle and the edge of the leaves. For the quilting around the leaves, switch to either free-motion quilting or hand quilting to echo quilt stitches in the body of the wreath. I also stitched in between the paired leaves to secure so that they wouldn't be too puffy after quilting.

For the remaining edges outside the wreath, you can continue with the quilting you are doing in the wreath or switch back to the spiral quilting with the walking foot, this time using the outer edge of the leaves as your guide. As you reach the edge of your quilt top, continue the quilting line out into the batting as a continuous circle. Fill in the corners one at a time, again using the left side of your presser foot as your guide between stitching lines.

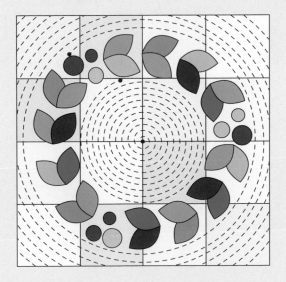

2. Place the 9″ circle or plate you used for the appliqué placement on one corner so that the edge of the plate touches two sides. Mark around this curve with a pencil or pen. This will become the cutting line when trimming to round the corner. *fig C*

3. Repeat for all 4 corners. Trim the quilted piece on the drawn lines.

4. Finish with binding cut on the bias (see Preparing Bias–Cut Binding, page 27) so that it will curve smoothly around the corners.

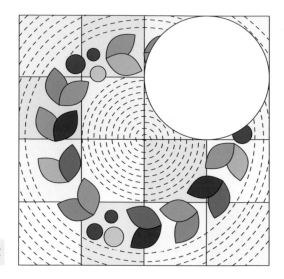

C

GATHER PATTERNS

Gather

Small Berry
Cut 3.

Gather

Large Berry
Cut 3.

Gather

Leaf
Cut 24.

Gather

Medium Berry
Cut 3.

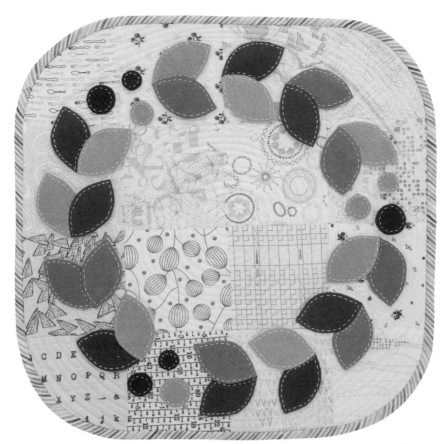

Gather table toppers

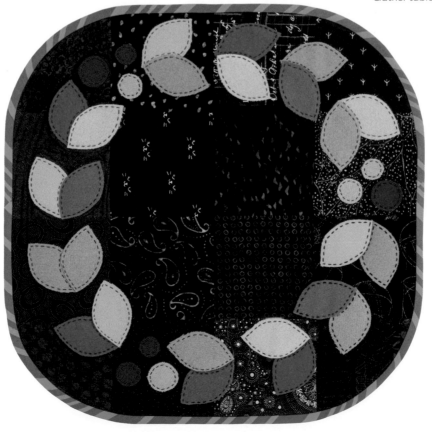

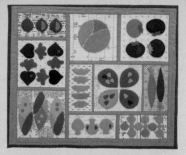

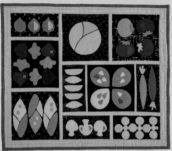

NOSH

FINISHED BLOCKS: 3″ × 6″ and 6″ × 6″
FINISHED QUILT: 21½″ × 18½″

Eat your veggies! Well, at least pretend to with this stylized version of veggies in Nosh. This project would work either as a kitchen or nook wallhanging or as a tray or tabletop quilt.

Materials

If you want your project to be entirely scrappy without repeating prints, use the highest number of suggested prints in the range and make sure all pieces are at least the minimum size.

Low-volume or dark prints: 8–10 assorted fabrics, minimum 6½″ × 6½″ square.
Or use alternate single-fabric background option: ⅓ yard.

Wool: 8–10 selections (6½″ × 8″ each) in a variety of colors, such as orange, red, gold, greens, light and dark brown, and magenta

Wool scraps: Minimum 2½″ × 2½″ squares in rust, purple, light pink, and lavender

Sashing: ¼ yard in light beige or taupe

Binding fabric: ¼ yard

Backing fabric: ¾ yard in red stripe

Batting: 24″ × 27″

> ### Project Particulars
> For my project as shown, I used felted wool from Local Farm Girl (see Resources, page 126) in the 03 and 04 range of the following colors: Bright Red, Red Lichen, Sunflower, Carrot, Green Lichen, Lettuce, Bright Green, Cosmos, Plum Pretty, and Warm Earth. I used a blanket stitch throughout in relatively matching colors in a variety of 12-weight cotton threads. I used a whipstitch in the smaller areas, such as the stems, and accented some areas with a backstitch (see Stitches, page 24).

Cutting

Low-volume or dark prints

- Cut 5 squares 6½″ × 6½″.

- Cut 5 rectangles 3½″ × 6½″.

Light beige or taupe cotton

Width of fabric (WOF) = 40″

- Cut 2 strips 1½″ × WOF; subcut *each* strip into:

  1 strip 1½″ × 19½″ for top and bottom borders

  1 strip 1½″ × 18½″ for side borders

- Cut 2 strips 1″ × WOF; subcut:

  1 strip 1″ × 16½″

  2 strips 1″ × 13″

  3 strips 1″ × 6½″

  1 strip 1″ × 3½″

- Cut 1 strip ¾″ × WOF; subcut 2 strips ¾″ × 6½″.

Binding

- Cut 3 strips 2¼″ × WOF.

Backing

- Cut 1 rectangle 26″ × 23″.

Construction

Seam allowances for piecing and construction are ¼″ throughout.

PREPARE THE APPLIQUÉ PIECES

Follow the general directions for preparing your appliqué pieces (page 22). Prepare the following number of pieces indicated on the pattern page (see Nosh Patterns, page 68).

BLOCK ASSEMBLY

1. Using the diagram and photos for placement suggestion, place the wool appliqué pieces on each background. Cabbage, tomatoes, beets, corn and artichokes use the 6″ square backgrounds; onions, peas, carrots, mushrooms, and brussels sprouts use the rectangles.

2. When you are satisfied with the placement, fuse the wool pieces to the backgrounds.

3. Hand stitch as desired.

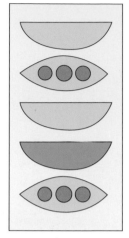

Peas

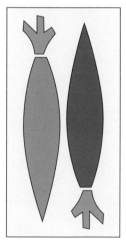

Carrots

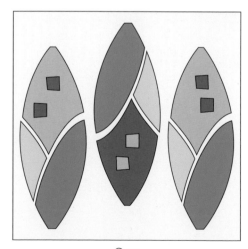

Corn

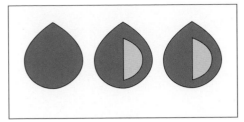

Onions

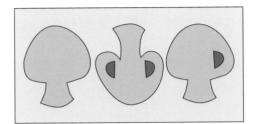

Mushrooms

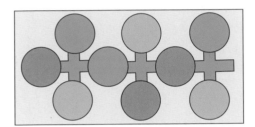

Brussels sprouts

Tomatoes

Beets

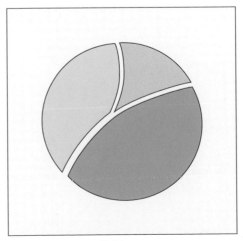

Cabbage

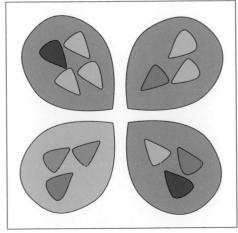

Artichokes

PROJECT ASSEMBLY

Because the sashing strips are thin, when possible, press the seams toward the blocks.

1. Referring to the diagrams, insert the sashing strips into each section to join the blocks. *fig A*

- 3 strips 1″ × 6½″ in the left column and top right sections

- 2 strips ¾″ × 6½″ in the middle right section

- 1 strip 1″ × 3½″ in the bottom right section

2. Join the sections on the right-hand side (top, middle, and bottom) adding 2 strips 1″ × 13″ between them. *fig B*

3. Add the 1″ × 16½″ strip between the left- and right-hand columns. *fig C*

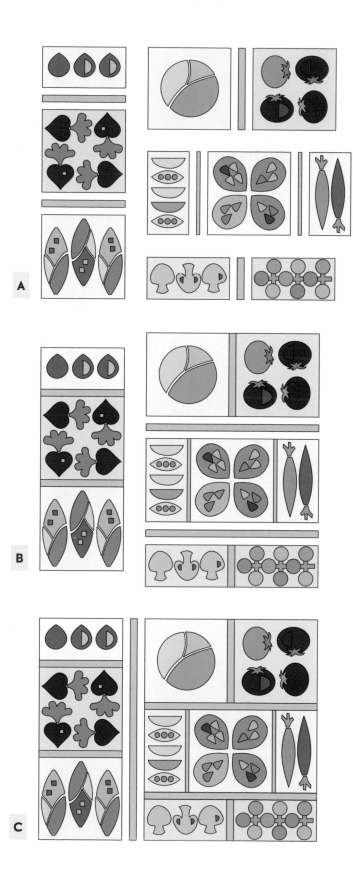

4. Add the top and bottom outer border strips 1½˝ × 19½˝. *fig D*

5. Complete the quilt top by adding the 2 side outer border strips 1½˝ × 18½˝. The pieced top should measure 21½˝ × 18½˝. *fig E*

FINISHING

Layer, quilt, and bind as desired.

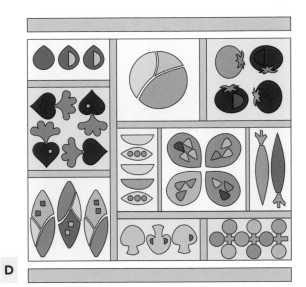

D

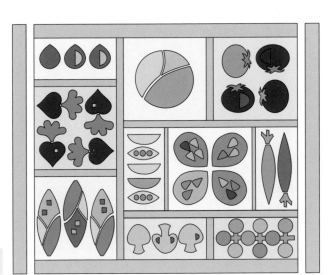

E

Quilting Idea

The quilting on this project was done on a longarm machine by Nikki Crisp. When quilting on a project of this size with small scale appliqué pieces, choose a complementary smaller scale quilting motif as well to balance your work.

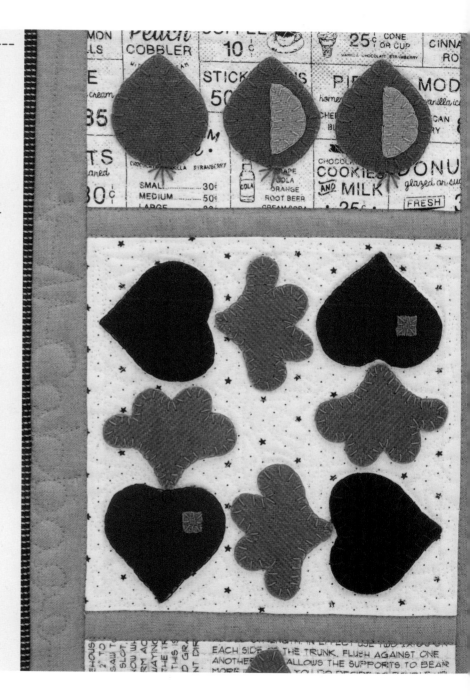

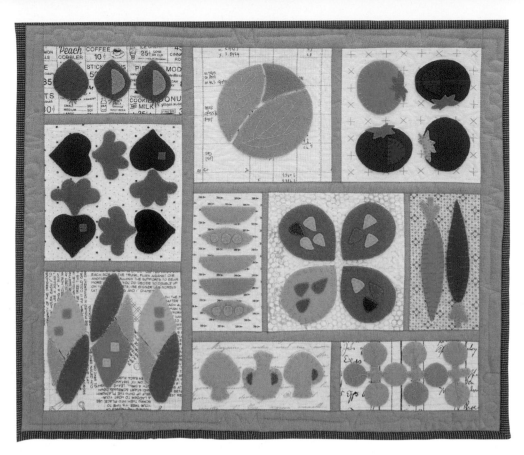

Nosh tray covers or wallhangings, quilting by Nikki Crisp

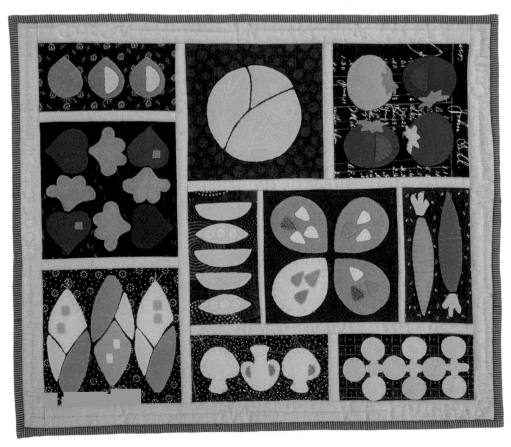

NOSH PATTERNS

Use this chart and the Nosh patterns to prepare the wool appliqué shapes.

Pattern label	Vegetable	Quantity
A	Onions	3
B	Cabbage	1
C	Tomatoes	4
D	Beets	4
E	Peas	5
F	Artichokes	4
G	Carrots	2
H	Corn	3
I	Mushrooms	3
J	Brussels sprouts	1

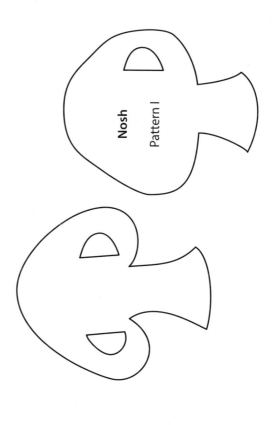

Nosh

Pattern I

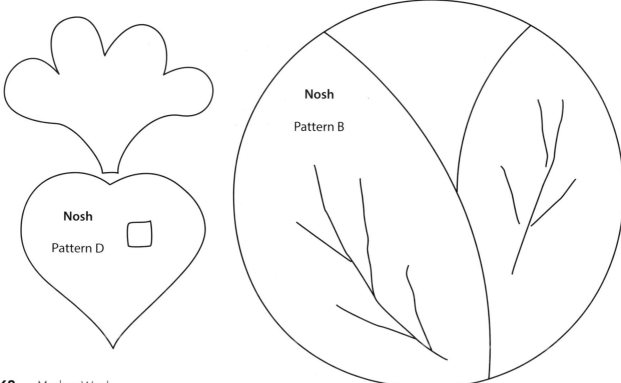

Nosh

Pattern D

Nosh

Pattern B

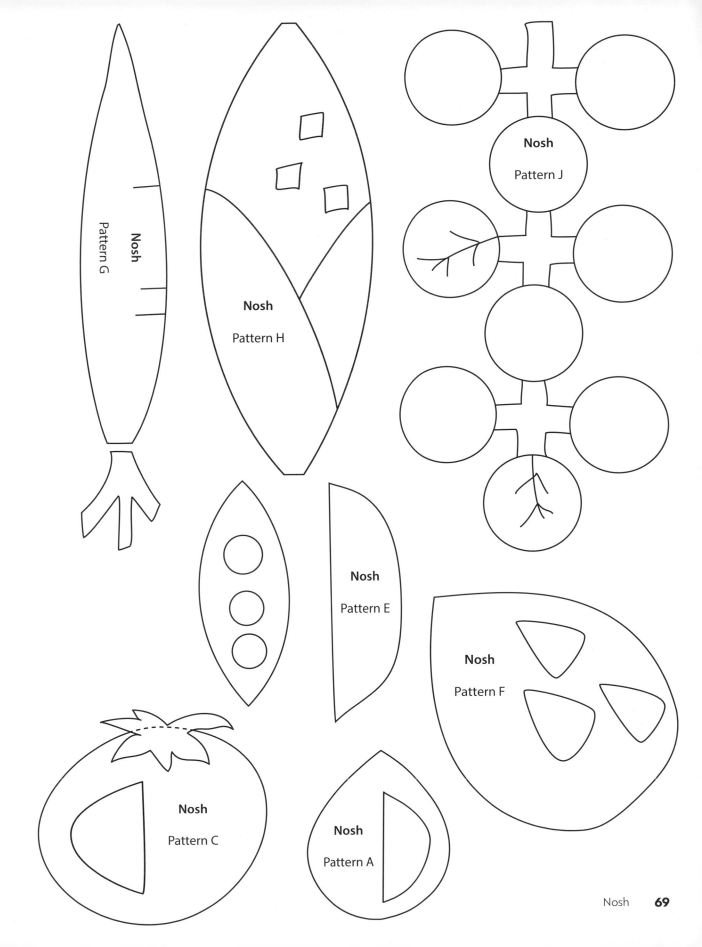

Nosh

Pattern G

Nosh

Pattern H

Nosh

Pattern J

Nosh

Pattern E

Nosh

Pattern F

Nosh

Pattern C

Nosh

Pattern A

Nosh **69**

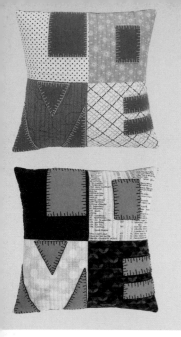

LOVE

FINISHED BLOCK: 6″ × 6″
FINISHED PILLOW: 12″ × 12″

Love is a pillow project that features a modern reverse alphabet image style. Whether printing or stitching, the subject of focus is usually the letter itself (see Push, page 86). But in this project, we're actually focusing on the background or negative space each letter creates. The Love pillow is a fun gift for your special someone—or pick some of your favorite fabrics and treat yourself!

Materials

Low-volume or dark prints: 2 fabrics, minimum 6½″ × 6½″ square. *Or use alternate single-fabric background option:* 1 fat quarter.

Gray prints: 2 fabrics, minimum 6½″ × 6½″ square each (No gray print needed for alternate background option.)

Pink solid: ¼ yard or 1 fat quarter for pillow back

Wool: 8″ × 10″ rectangle in pink

Scrap fabric or muslin: 15″ × 15″ square for back of quilted pillow front (This will be inside the pillow and will not be visible in the finished project.)

Batting: 15″ × 15″

Pillow form: 12″ × 12″

Cutting

Low-volume or dark prints

- Cut 2 squares 6½″ × 6½″.
  Or use alternate single-fabric background option:
  1 square 12½″ × 12½″.

Gray prints

- Cut 2 squares 6½″ × 6½″.

Pink solid

- Cut 2 rectangles 8½″ × 12½″.

Project Particulars

For my project as shown I used XoticFelt, a bamboo felt blend from National Nonwovens (see Resources, page 126) in Passion Flower. For the appliqué, I used an alternating blanket stitch (see Stitches, page 24) in 12-weight perle cotton.

Construction

Seam allowances for piecing and construction are ¼" throughout.

PREPARE THE APPLIQUÉ PIECES

1. Cut a piece of fusible web the same size as your piece of wool (8" × 10"). Trace Triangle A (see Love Pattern, page 76) onto the paper side of the fusible web in one corner. Apply the fusible web to the back of the wool.

2. Cut 1 rectangle 3" × 4" for the L block.

3. Cut 1 rectangle 2" × 3" for the O block.

4. Cut 2 rectangles 2" × 4" for the V block. Following the illustration, cut each diagonally, corner to corner, but in opposite directions. (*Note: You will have 2 leftover triangles.*) **fig A**

5. Cut out the traced Triangle A for the V block.

6. Cut 2 rectangles 1¼" × 3" for the E block.

A

BLOCK ASSEMBLY

If you are using the single-fabric option, divide the large square into 4 "blocks" by making a vertical and then a horizontal fold. Use the fold lines to help with appliqué placement. Seam allowances will only be around the outside edge.

1. Following the photo, place the wool appliqué shapes on each 6½" × 6½" square to create the letters, leaving ⅜" from each edge of the background uncovered. An easy way to do this is to lay your ruler ⅜" over the edge of the background block as you position your appliqué pieces so that you can avoid getting your pieces caught in the seam allowance. **fig B**

2. When you are satisfied with the placement, fuse the wool pieces to the backgrounds.

3. Hand stitch as desired.

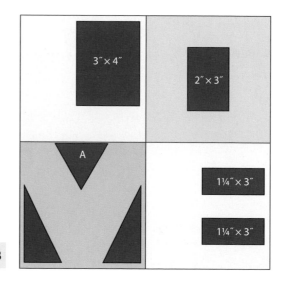

B

PROJECT ASSEMBLY

Follow the arrows for pressing direction.

1. Sew the blocks into rows.

2. Sew the rows together. The pieced top should measure 12½″ × 12½″. **fig C**

3. Layer the pieced project top, the 15″ × 15″ square of batting, and the 15″ × 15″ square of scrap fabric or muslin into a quilt sandwich. The pieced top is slightly smaller than the batting and backing.

4. Baste the three layers together using your preferred method. I chose to use basting spray for this project.

5. Quilt as desired.

6. Trim the quilted pillow top to 12½″ × 12½″ square.

C

Straight-Line Quilting with the Walking Foot

The quilting motif on my project was achieved using the walking foot on my sewing machine. Most machines come with a walking foot attachment or an integrated dual-feed foot that does the same thing. The walking foot works by pulling multiple layers of fabric, in this case our quilt sandwich, under the presser foot. Pressure is applied to both the top and the bottom of the fabric layers using the teeth in the feed dogs and the foot itself.

For my project, I decided on alternating horizontal and vertical quilting lines in each block. I first stitched directly in the seams in both directions between the four blocks (referred to as stitch in the ditch) to stabilize each section. Then one block at a time, I began stitching back and forth using the width of my presser foot to measure stitching line to stitching line. In this case, that spacing is about ½″ between lines.

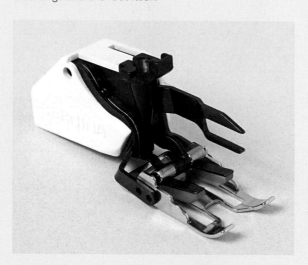

I stopped at the end of each line, beyond the edge of the quilt block out in the extra batting/backing, or when the stitching line met an appliqué piece. With the needle down, I pivoted the piece, stitched over a few stitches (mine needed 4 or 5 stitches because of my stitch length), put the needle back down, turned the piece, and started stitching the next line in the opposite direction. The turnaround stitches out in the batting will get trimmed off in the finishing steps.

If your presser foot doesn't conveniently match the line spacing you are looking for, you can mark your stitching lines with any method you prefer before beginning your quilting. Good choices for straight-line quilting like this would be to use a Hera Marker or low-tack quilt marking tape.

FINISHING

1. Lay the 2 backing fabric rectangles 8½" × 12" wrong sides up on your pressing surface.

2. Fold over one of the 12" sides ¼" and press. Fold the same edge over again ¼" and press again. Repeat for the second rectangle. *fig D*

3. Using a straight stitch on your machine, stitch slightly less than ¼" down the full length of the folded edge to secure.

4. Lay your 12½" square quilted and trimmed pillow top right side up on your work surface. Place a prepared backing rectangle on the pillow top, wrong side facing up, top edge aligned to pillow front, and folded edge horizontal across the pillow top. *fig E*

D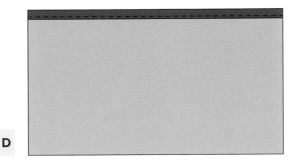

E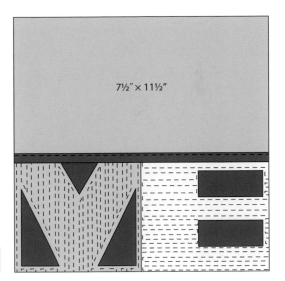

7½" × 11½"

5. Place the remaining prepared backing rectangle, wrong side facing up, bottom and sides aligned to pillow front, and folded edge horizontal across the pillow top and overlapping the first pillow backing. Place securing pins all the way around. *fig F*

6. Stitch all the way around the outside edge using ¼" seam allowance.

7. Trim the corners being sure not to snip into the sewing line. Turn the pillow cover right side out. Carefully push out the corners using a turning tool or dull pencil. Press to flatten out the seams and insert the 12" pillow form.

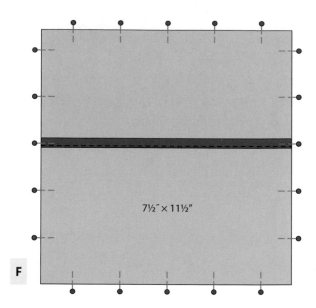

7½" × 11½"

F

LOVE PATTERN

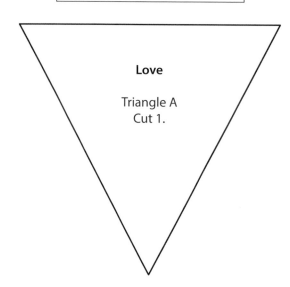

Love

Triangle A
Cut 1.

Love pillows

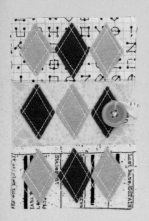
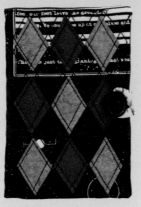

PLAY

FINISHED NEEDLEBOOK: 4″ × 6″

It seems it should be a requirement for a book on wool hand appliqué to include a needlebook project. A needlebook is so handy and portable to keep all our needles where we can find them! This little needlebook is as simple as it is satisfying and showcases the wool in two different ways—in the appliqué and as the pages of the needlebook. Play would also be a great companion piece to go with a Push pincushion (page 86) for a special sewing friend.

Materials

A fat eighth can measure 9″ × 21″–22″ or 11″ × 18″.

Low-volume or dark prints: 3 strips 2½″ wide, minimum 8½″ length.
Or use alternate single-fabric background option: 1 fat eighth.

Coordinating print: 1 fat eighth

Wool: 2 selections (8″ × 9″ each) in teal and bright pink
or 2 colors that complement the prints

Batting: 6½″ × 8½″

Grosgrain ribbon or twill tape: ⅜″ wide, 12″ length, for button loop and scissor loop

Decorative button: ¾″ round or similar

*For decorative use only; should not be used to establish actual measurements.

Project Particulars

For my project as shown, I used felted wool from Andover Fabrics' teal and bright pink color selections from a 10″ precut stack of WoolWerks Ice and a bright green from WoolWerks Fresh. The cotton fabrics used in this project are also from Andover Fabrics; the feature prints are Declassified by Giuseppe Ribaudo (a.k.a. Giucy Giuce) from Andover Fabrics and Handiwork by Alison Glass. Embellishment Measuring Tape Ribbon* is from Galaxy Notions. For the stitching, I used a simple running stitch (see Stitches, page 24) in either black or white 12-weight cotton thread.

Cutting

Low-volume or dark prints:

- Cut 3 strips 2½″ × 8½″ for cover.
  Or use alternate single-fabric background option:
  1 rectangle 6½″ × 8½″.

Coordinating print:

- Cut 1 rectangle 6½″ × 8½″ for lining.

Teal wool:

- Cut 1 rectangle 5″ × 7″ for book page.

Bright pink wool:

- Cut 1 rectangle 4½″ × 6″ for book page.
  Measure and mark a point 1½″ from each of
  top 2 corners in both directions. Align ruler
  on 2 marked points and cut to trim.

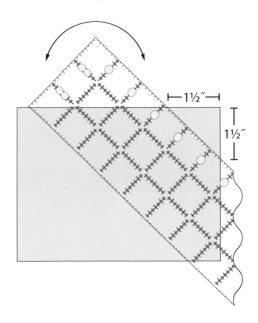

Grosgrain ribbon or twill tape:

- Cut 1 piece 3½″ length for button loop.

- Cut 1 piece 2″ length for scissor loop.

Construction

*Seam allowances for piecing and construction are
¼″ throughout.*

PREPARE THE APPLIQUÉ DIAMONDS

Follow the general directions in Appliqué Basics
(page 22) to prepare your appliqué pieces.
Prepare 7 teal diamonds and 4 bright pink
diamonds (see Play Pattern, page 85).

PIECE THE BOOK COVER

*If you are using the single-fabric option for the
background, continue to Project Assembly
(next page).*

1. Arrange the 3 fabric strips 2½″ × 8½″ in an
order of your liking.

2. Join the 3 strips together along the long edges
to create a strip set that measures 6½″ × 8½″.
Press the seams in any direction.

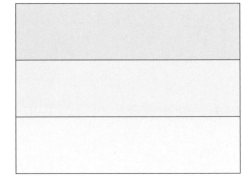

PROJECT ASSEMBLY

1. Place the 6½″ × 8½″ rectangle of batting on your work surface. Place the 6½″ × 8½″ cover rectangle on top, right side up. *fig A*

2. Fold the 3½″–long piece of twill tape in half to form a loop and position in the center on the left side of the strip set. Align the cut ends with the outside fabric edge and pin to secure. *fig B*

3. Place the 6½″ × 8½″ lining rectangle on top, right sides together. Pin through all three layers all the way around. This is the mini quilt sandwich.

4. Sew all the way around the rectangle, leaving a 2½″ opening on the bottom. *fig C*

5. Before turning right side out, snip the corners to remove bulk, being sure not to snip into the stitched seam. Turn the mini quilt sandwich right side out through the opening. Use a dull stylus, knitting needle, or eraser end of a pencil to help push out the seams fully.

6. Press the mini quilt sandwich from both sides. Turn the raw edges of the opening inward and close with a small whipstitch or slip stitch (see Stitches, page 24) in matching thread. *fig D*

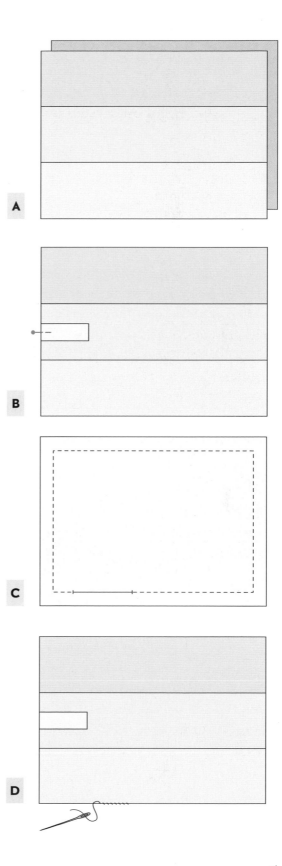

A

B

C

D

APPLIQUÉ AND QUILTING

1. With the button loop on the right side and interior facing up, fold the cover in half, left side to right. This will be the same as the finished orientation. Press the folded edge with the iron to give yourself a registration mark for arranging the appliqué pieces on what will be the front cover. *fig E*

2. Open the book cover and place it flat, face up on your work surface, button loop to the left. Arrange 5 teal wool diamonds and 4 bright pink wool diamonds on the front cover—the right-hand side. The side points of the end diamonds should be ¼″ away from the center fold on the left and ¼″ from the right outside edge.

3. Fuse the wool appliqué pieces into place. *fig F*

4. With an acrylic ruler and a Hera Marker, mark 60° angle lines on the outside cover as shown. *fig G*

5. Using a running or quilting stitch, stitch through all three layers of your quilt sandwich on all the marked lines.

Combo Quilting

The stitching in this project is doing double duty; it is securing the appliqué pieces and it's completing the quilting at the same time. I used a running stitch and you could choose to do this by machine as well. If stitching by hand, change to a sturdy needle with a sharp tip, such as a utility needle or Sashiko needle, for ease of going through all three layers.

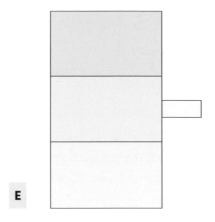

E

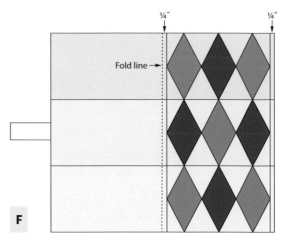

F

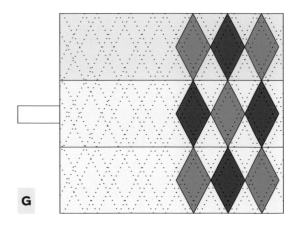

G

Using 12-Weight Thread in Your Machine

Heavier 12-weight thread on a spool can be used for hand stitching or in your domestic machine. If the 12-weight thread is wound in a ball without a spool, it is not suitable for use in your machine.

Thread your machine as normal with 12-weight thread on top and 40-weight thread in the bobbin. Use a size 100/16 or 90/14 topstitch needle in the machine. You may find that you want to lengthen the stitches for visual impact as well. Go slowly but stitch as normal.

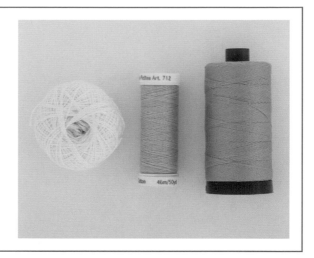

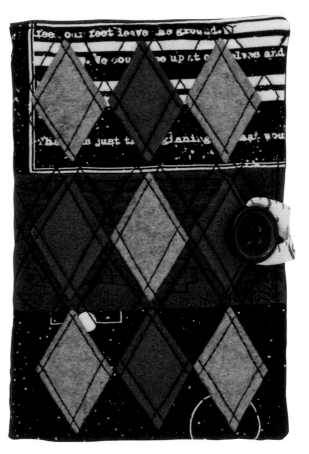

Play needlebooks

FINISHING

1. After the stitching is completed, we're ready to add the finishing touches. Open the needlebook on your work surface, inside facing up. Place the teal wool rectangle 5″ × 7″ in the center.

2. Layer the wool rectangle 4½″ × 6″ with cropped corners on top of the teal rect-angle. Align the bottom edges of the wool pieces. Either by machine or by hand, stitch down the spine of the book, securing the pages and the cover. *fig H*

3. Add the remaining teal diamond appliqués to the inside cropped pages. Fuse and stitch as desired. *fig I*

4. Add the 2½″ length of twill tape to the back inside cover. Hand stitch it into place for the scissor loop. *fig J*

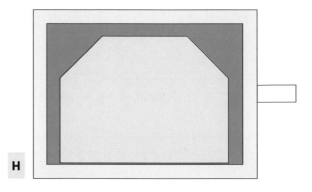

H

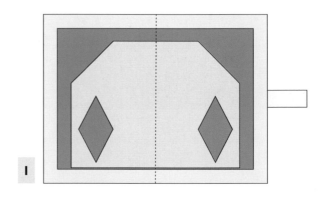

I

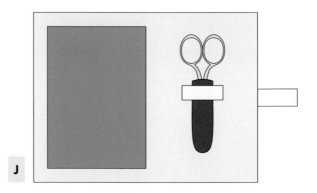

J

5. To finish, add the button to the front cover. Fill the pages with needles and you're ready to go! *fig K*

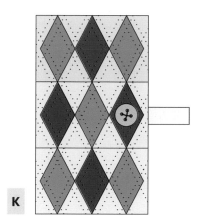

K

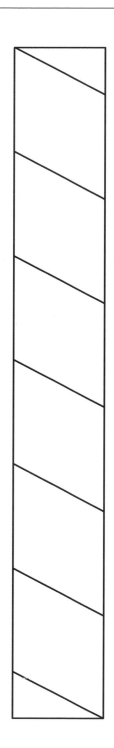

PUSH

FINISHED PINCUSHION: 4″ round × 2″ tall

As a quilter and sewist, I don't think it's possible to have too many pincushions, especially if they are monogrammed! The Push pincushions are inspired by retro typewriter keys and I must say it's hard to stop at making just one. They make a great personalized gift for sewing friends and the fabric combos are limitless.

Materials

A fat eighth can measure 9″ × 21″–22″ or 11″ × 18″.

Low-volume or dark print: 1 fat eighth

Coordinating print: 1 fat eighth

Wool: 1 square 5″ × 5″ in color of your choice to match your fabric selection

Scrap fabric or muslin: 1 square 8″ × 8″ for lining to hold filling inside

Batting: 1 square 8″ × 8″

Grosgrain or ribbon twill tape: ⅝″ wide, 13″ length, for side embellishment

Pincushion filling: Your choice (see Pincushion Filling Ideas, page 88)

Cutting

Make a circle template from the Push pattern (page 93) to cut the pincushion top and bottom.

Low-volume or dark print

- Cut 1 strip 1½″ × 13″ for pincushion side.

- Cut 4½″-diameter circle for pincushion top.

Coordinating print

- Cut 1 strip 1½″ × 13″ for pincushion side.

- Cut 4½″-diameter circle for pincushion bottom.

Project Particulars

For my project as shown, I used felted wool from Andover Fabrics, making my color selections from a 10″ precut stack of WoolWerks Merry & Bright for the monogram initials. The cotton fabrics used in this project are also from Andover Fabrics; the feature prints are Declassified by Giuseppe Ribaudo (a.k.a. Giucy Giuce) from Andover Fabrics and Handiwork by Alison Glass. Embellishment Measuring Tape Ribbon* is from Galaxy Notions (see Resources, page 126). For the stitching, I used a simple running stitch (see Stitches, page 24) in either black or white 12-weight cotton thread.

* This twill tape that resembles a measuring tape is for decorative use only and should not be used to establish actual measurements.

Pincushion Filling Ideas

Pincushions have been around for centuries and the preferred stuffing inside has changed over time. Antique pincushions have been found to contain old pencil shavings, sawdust, horsehair, wool roving, scrap fabric bits, and even old broken sewing needles!

The choice is yours. Consider these ideas:

- Poly-Fil Poly-Beads (by Fairfield)
- Fiberfill stuffing
- Scrap pieces of batting (especially wool batting)
- Wool trimmings from other projects
- Wool roving
- Crushed walnut shells
- Fine sand
- Dried lavender
- Yellow split peas or lentils
- Smashed coffee beans
- Fine-grade steel wool
- A mix of things

I like to use crushed walnut shells in a bundle of scrap muslin and wool batting for weight and stability. The muslin helps contain the dust in the filling that might leak out of the weave of the cotton fabrics.

To do this, take an 8″ × 8″ square of muslin and poke it into the opening of the constructed pincushion with the corners sticking out of the opening creating a little pocket inside. Using a small funnel or cup, pour the crushed walnut shells into the pocket area.

When it's as full as you would like, twist the bundle ends and tuck them inside the pincushion. Tuck scrap wool batting or fiberfill stuffing into the remaining space around the bundle and to even out the surface of the pincushion. Whipstitch the small opening of the pincushion to close.

Construction

Seam allowances for piecing and construction are ¼" throughout.

PREPARE THE APPLIQUÉ PINCUSHION TOP

1. Follow the general directions in Appliqué Basics (page 22) to prepare the monogram initial of your choosing. See Push Patterns (pages 93–97).

2. Center your initial on the top fabric 4½" circle. Fuse into place.

3. Hand stitch as desired. *fig A*

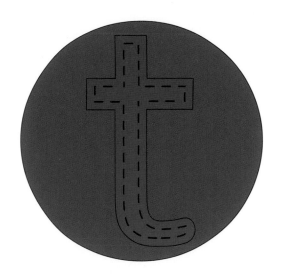

A

PIECE THE PINCUSHION SIDES

1. Place the 2 fabric strips 1½" × 13" right sides together and sew on the long edge to join the strips. Press the seam in any direction. *fig B*

B

2. Center the 13" length of ribbon on top of the seamline and secure with a few pins. *fig C*

C

3. Top stitch down the length of the ribbon on both edges. The side piece will now measure 2½" × 13".

4. Fold the side strip short end to short end, right sides together. Sew the two short ends together to create a loop. Press the seam open to help with the bulk of the ribbon. The loop will be inside out at this point, with the right sides facing in. *fig D*

D

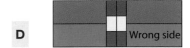

Wrong side

PROJECT ASSEMBLY

1. Place the prepared side loop on your work surface with the fabric strip matching the top fabric at the top. *fig E*

2. Match the top 4½″ circle fabric to the identical fabric strip on the loop (see project photos, page 87). Align the side seam with the top of the initial.

3. Pin all the way around, easing the top circle and side loop together. *fig F*

4. Sew all the way around the circle, easing the fabric under the presser foot slowly. Use a stylus to help guide the fabric. Lift the presser foot occasionally and readjust the fabric as you go. *fig G*

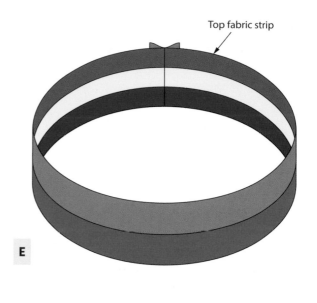

Top fabric strip

E

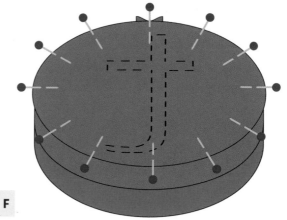

F

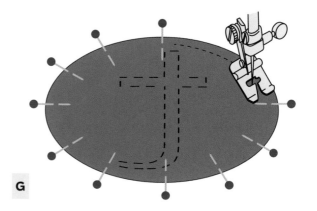

G

5. Place the joined sections from Step 4 on your work surface, top circle flat on the work surface, creating a little bowl. Lay the bottom fabric 4½″ circle on top, right side facing down.

6. Pin all the way around again, easing the bottom circle and loop together.

7. Repeat Step 4, sewing around the circle leaving a 2″–3″ opening which you will need for turning and to add the filling. *fig H*

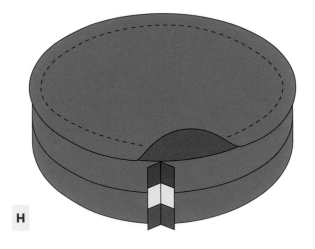

H

8. Before turning right side out, snip the seam allowance all the way around the top and bottom circles being sure not to snip into the stitched seams. Turn the pincushion right side out through the opening. Use a dull stylus, knitting needle, or eraser end of a pencil to help push out the seams fully.

9. Fill the pincushion with filling of your choice (see Pincushion Filling Ideas, page 88).

10. With matching thread, hand stitch the opening closed with a small whipstitch or slip stitch (see Stitches, page 24).

Push pincushions

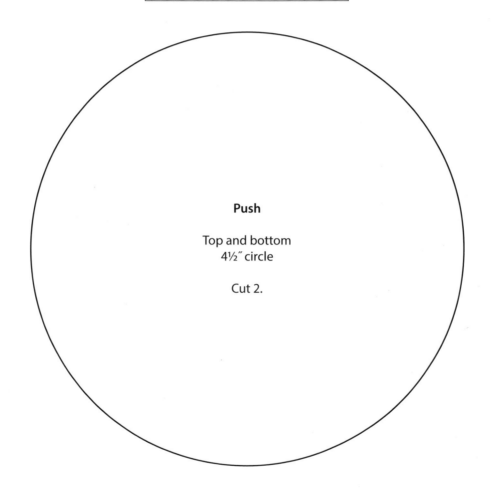

PUSH PATTERNS

Push

Top and bottom
4½″ circle

Cut 2.

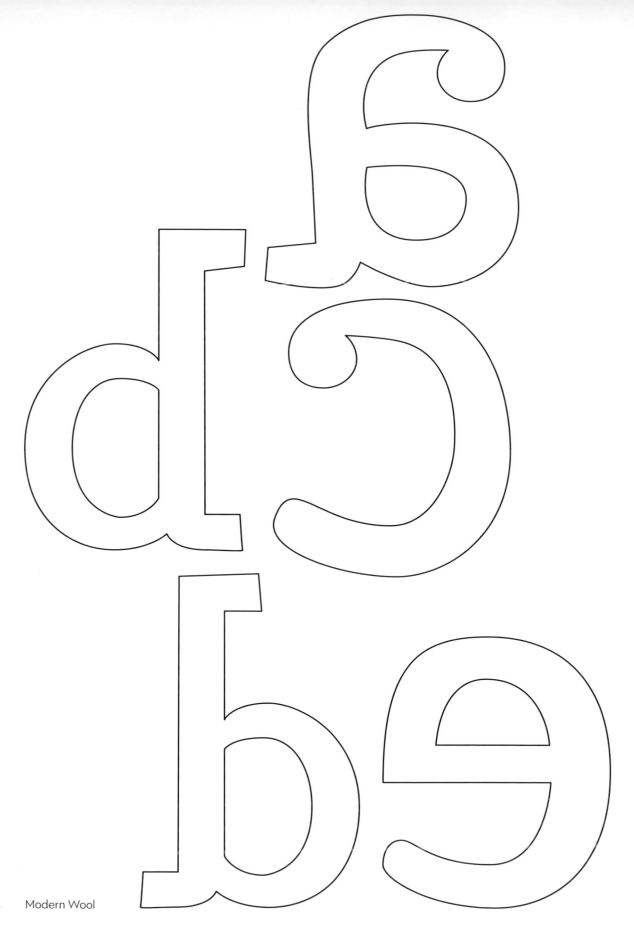

GROW

FINISHED SLEEVE: 10½″ × 8″

While book covers are out these days, tablet reader covers are in. Grow is a stylish and simple envelope sleeve to protect your reader when not in use. I patterned Grow to fit my 8″ × 10″ touchscreen tablet. You can adjust the size if you want, but this sleeve is roomy enough to accommodate a slight difference in sizes as is.

Materials

If you want your project to be entirely scrappy without repeating prints, use the highest number of suggested prints in the range and make sure all pieces are at least the minimum size.

A fat eighth can measure 9″ × 21″–22″ or 11″ × 18″.

Low-volume or dark prints: 4–6 assorted fabrics, minimum 3″ × 5¾″ rectangle
Or use alternate single-fabric background option: 1 fat eighth.

Coordinating print: 1 fat eighth

Lining print: 1 fat quarter *or* 1 fat eighth that measures 11″ × 18″

Wool: 4–6 selections (6½″ × 4″ each) in a variety of greens, golds, and plum

Batting: 11″ × 16″

Twill tape: ⅝″ wide, 3″ length, for loop tab

Cutting

Low-volume or dark back-ground print

- Cut 6 rectangles 3″ × 5¾″ for sleeve cover.
  Or use alternate single-fabric background option:
  1 rectangle 8″ × 11″.

Coordinating print

- Cut 1 rectangle 8½″ × 11″ for sleeve back.

Lining print

- Cut 1 rectangle 11″ × 16″.

Project Particulars

For my project as shown, I used felted wool from Andover Fabrics, making color selections from a 10″ precut stack of WoolWerks Fresh and WoolWerks Fire. The cotton fabrics used in this project are also from Andover Fabrics and feature prints from Handiwork by Alison Glass, along with a few other scraps on the front cover backgrounds. Embellishment Measuring Tape Ribbon is from Galaxy Notions (see Resources, page 126). For the stitching, I used a variety of stitches including whipstitch, cross-stitch, angled blanket stitch, seed stitch, and French knots (see Stitches, page 24) in 12-weight cotton thread.

Construction

Seam allowances for piecing and construction are ¼″ throughout.

PIECE THE BOOK COVER

If using the alternate single-fabric background, skip to Prepare the Appliqué Pieces (below).

1. Arrange the 6 fabric rectangles 3″ × 5¾″ in an order of your liking.

2. Join the rectangles in rows of 2 and then join the 3 rows together along the long edges to create a background block that will measure 8″ × 11″. Press the seams in any direction. *fig A*

PREPARE THE APPLIQUÉ PIECES

1. Follow the general directions in Appliqué Basics (page 22) to prepare your appliqué pieces. Prepare pieces 1–16 (see Grow Patterns, page 105).

2. Using the diagram and photos for placement suggestion, place the wool appliqué pieces on the background rectangle. *fig B*

3. When you are satisfied with the placement, fuse the wool pieces to the background.

4. Hand stitch as desired.

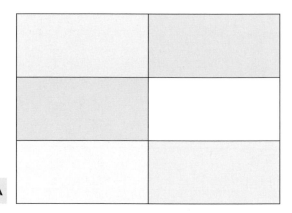

A

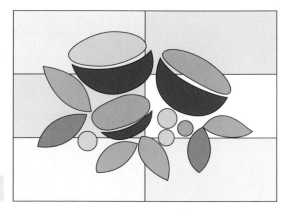

B

PROJECT ASSEMBLY

1. Place the outside back cover coordinating print fabric 8½″ × 11″ rectangle and the appliquéd front cover right sides together and sew together along the bottom edge. Press the seam toward back cover fabric. *fig C*

2. Place the 11″ × 16″ rectangle of batting on your work surface. Place the 11″ × 16″ lining rectangle on top, right side facing up.

3. Fold the 3″–long piece of twill tape in half to form a loop and position in the upper right–hand corner ½″ away from the corner. Align the cut ends with the outside fabric edge and pin to secure. *fig D*

4. Place the cover on top, right sides together, with the appliquéd side of the cover on the left. This will also be the opposite end from the twill tape loop tab. Pin through all three layers all the way around. This is the mini quilt sandwich.

C

D

5. Sew all the way around the rectangle, leaving a 4″ opening on the bottom right unsewn. *fig E*

6. Before turning right side out, snip the corners to remove bulk, being sure not to snip into the stitched seam. Turn the mini quilt sandwich right side out through the opening. Use a dull stylus, knitting needle, or eraser end of a pencil to help push out the seams fully.

7. Press the mini quilt sandwich from both sides. Turn the raw edges of the opening inward and close with a small whipstitch or slip stitch (see Stitches, page 24) in matching thread. *fig F*

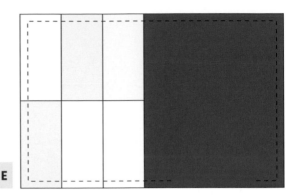

E

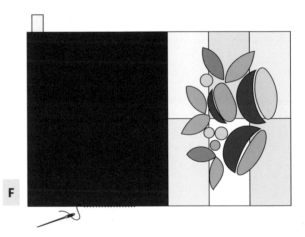

F

QUILTING AND FINISHING

1. Place a few basting pins across the surface of the cover to stabilize. Quilt as desired.

Matchstick Quilting with the Walking Foot

For my project as shown, I chose to echo quilt around the appliqué shapes and then finish the remaining areas with a matchstick quilting motif.

Matchstick quilting gets its name for the straight lines of quilting, literally about a matchstick's width apart. It's easy to do with the walking foot of your domestic machine and creates a dense evenly-quilted surface design.

Mark the initial stitch line with a Hera Marker and a couple more across the piece to act as registration marks. By giving your eye some registration marks to follow, it will help keep your quilting lines straight without having to mark every stitch line.

Start in the center by stitching on the first center marked line and work outward toward the ends.

When you reach the end of each quilted line, stop with needle down, pivot and take 2 stitches over, put the needle down again, and pivot to return in the opposite direction.

2. Fold the completed sleeve so that the cover faces up and the lining fabric is on the inside. The front cover comes just up to the twill tape loop tab, creating a ½″ overlap to show the inside lining fabric of the completed sleeve. Pin or clip the sides together to temporarily secure.

3. With coordinating 8-weight perle cotton thread for strength, whipstitch (see Stitches, page 24) both sides to finish the sleeve. *fig G*

G

Grow tablet reader sleeves

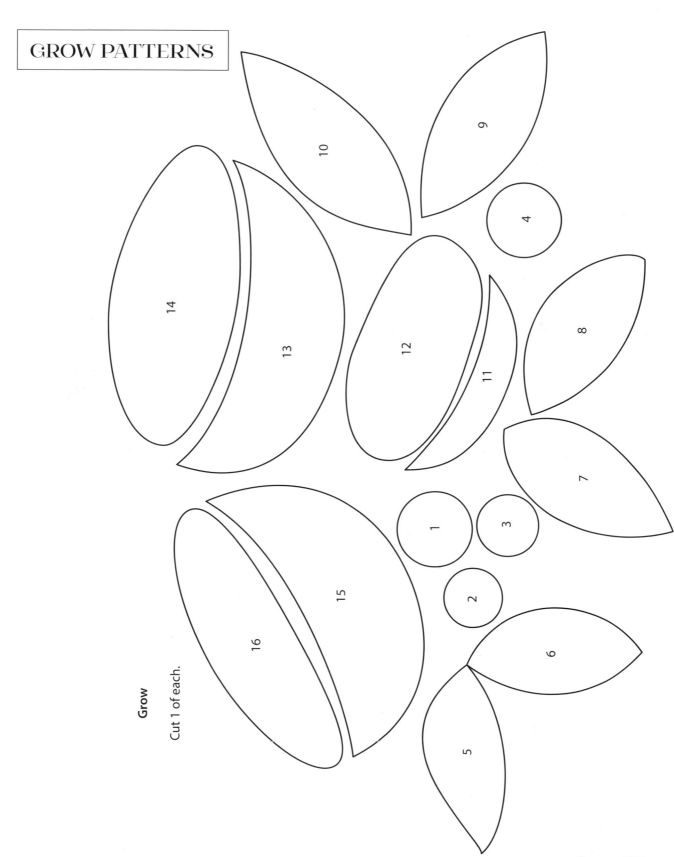

Grow

Cut 1 of each.

DWELL

FINISHED WALLHANGING: 12″ × 12″
(optional: 6″ × 18″ and 12″ × 18″)

As with any pattern you are following, you should always feel free to make it unique and make it your own! Dwell is a house sampler that encourages you to mix and match a variety of house blocks to make your project. Stitches can be plain or fancy, and can add details like windows, doors, chimneys, flower boxes, house numbers, names, or dates. You can be intentional and fussy cut your background fabrics to add print elements to pop into your windows, add bits of wool scraps for extra details ... the possibilities are endless.

Materials

The following materials will make a sampler of 4 dwell blocks—3 house and 1 heart block—in a 2 × 2 setting.

Low-volume or dark prints: 4 fabrics, minimum 6½″ × 6½″ square. *Or use alternate single-fabric background option:* ⅜ yard.

Wool: 10–14 selections (6½″ × 4″ each) in a variety of blues and golds for houses; pink, red, and magenta for heart

Binding fabric: ¼ yard

Backing fabric: 1 fat quarter (18″ × 20″–22″)

Batting: 17″ × 17″

Cutting

Low-volume or dark prints

- Cut 4 squares 6½″ × 6½″.
  Or use alternate single-fabric background option:
  1 square 12½″ × 12½″.

Binding

- Cut 2 strips 2¼″ × WOF.

Backing

- Cut 1 square 17″ × 17″.

Project Particulars

For my project as shown, I used felted wool from Local Farm Girl (see Resources, page 126) in the 03 and 04 range of the following colors: Cosmos, Bright Red, Sunflower, Colorado Sky, and Turquoise. For the stitching, I used a variety of stitches in a wide variety of colored threads to add interest. All threads were 12–weight cotton.

Construction

Seam allowances for piecing and construction are ¼" throughout.

PREPARE THE APPLIQUÉ PIECES

Follow the general directions in Appliqué Basics (page 22) to prepare your appliqué pieces. Prepare the number of pieces necessary to complete your chosen blocks. (See Dwell Patterns, pages 111–115.) You have the option of reversing the B block house. Use the B block roof reversed pattern for a reversed version.

BLOCK ASSEMBLY

1. Place the wool appliqué pieces on each of 4 background squares. Be sure not to place appliqué pieces in the seam allowances. For help with appliqué placement, align a ruler ¼" over the edge to cover the seam allowance while placing your appliqué pieces.

If you are using the single-fabric option, divide the large square into 4 "blocks" by making a vertical and then a horizontal fold. Use the fold lines to help with appliqué placement. *fig A*

2. When you are satisfied with the placement, fuse the wool pieces to the backgrounds.

3. Hand stitch as desired.

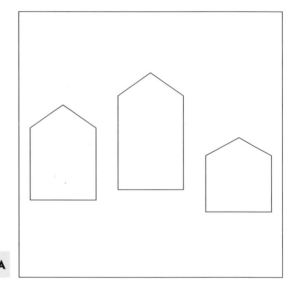

A

PROJECT ASSEMBLY

1. Sew the blocks into rows.

2. Sew the rows together. The pieced top should measure 12½" × 12½".

FINISHING

Layer and quilt as desired. Finish with binding.

Adding Triangle Tabs for a Hanging Dowel

An easy alternative to adding a full hanging sleeve on small projects like this is to add corner triangle tabs sewn into the binding for hanging with a wooden dowel rod. This technique will keep the finished quilt project flat and straight for hanging on the wall.

This method works best when attaching the binding completely by machine, topstitching the binding on the front of the quilt instead of hand-stitching to the back (see *Tip: Binding Completely by Machine, page 30*).

There are lots of options of hangers to choose from: thin wooden dowels, skewers, or even chop sticks. Wooden dowel rods are easy to find at any craft store that carries wood craft products or even at your local hardware store. Look for wood dowels ¼" thick and cut to whatever length you need. For Dwell made as shown, you will need a 12" piece of wood dowel.

It's also a good idea to attach tabs to all 4 corners at the same time. This way you can add another dowel to the bottom to keep the project hanging straight and flat to the wall.

1. To make the corner tabs, cut 4 squares 4" × 4". Fold each square in half, corner to corner. *fig A*

2. Baste stitch the folded triangles, either by hand or machine, onto all 4 corners on the back side of the quilt, aligning the raw edges with the sides of the quilt. *fig B*

3. Attach prepared binding strips to the back of the quilt using the all-machine method, stitching over the basted triangles to secure them in the seam underneath the binding strip. Flip the binding over to the front and secure with a stitch of your choice to the front of the quilt.

4. To hang, just insert the wooden dowel ends into the pockets created by the corner triangles at the top. Insert another dowel in the bottom tabs if desired. The dowel can be easily hung over a nail or two on the wall. It will be behind the quilt and completely out of sight.

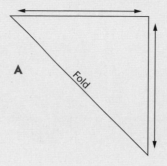

A

Fold

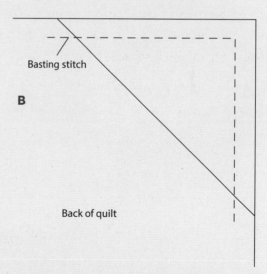

B

Basting stitch

Back of quilt

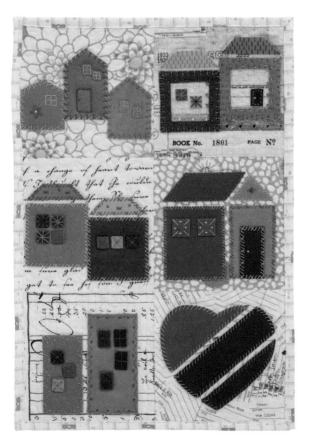

Dwell wallhangings

DWELL PATTERNS

Dwell

A block

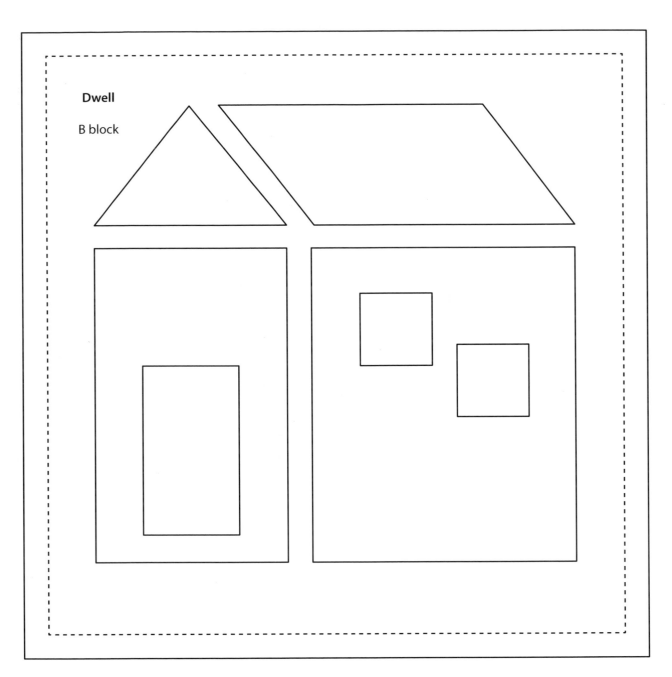

Dwell

B block

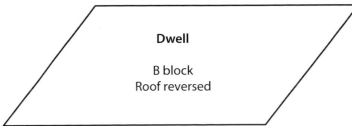

Dwell

B block
Roof reversed

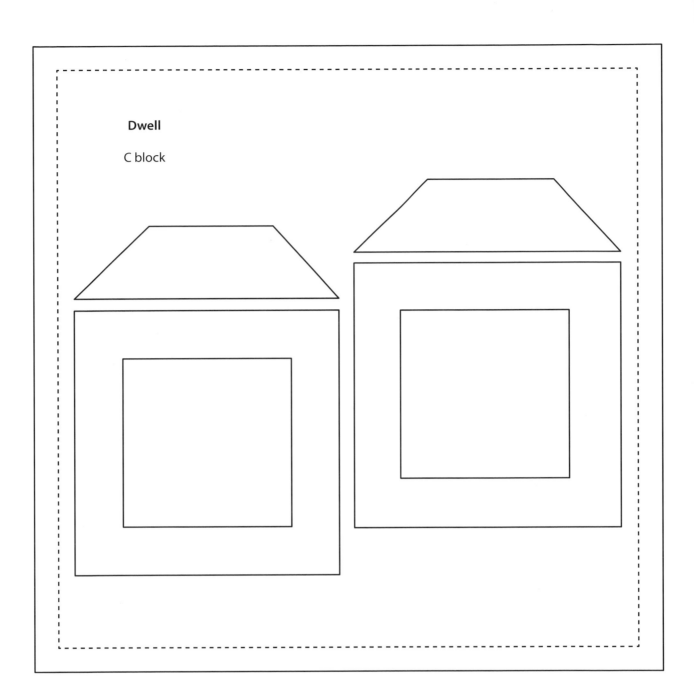

Dwell

C block

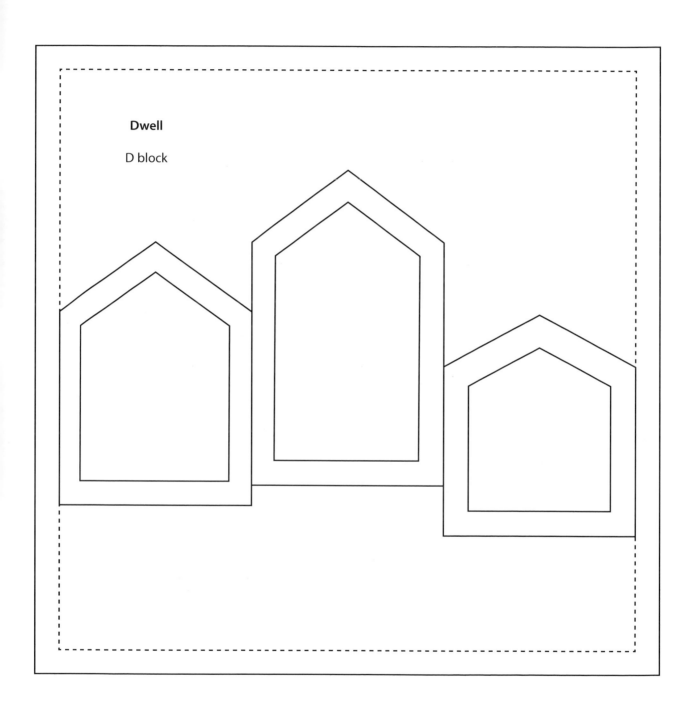

Dwell

D block

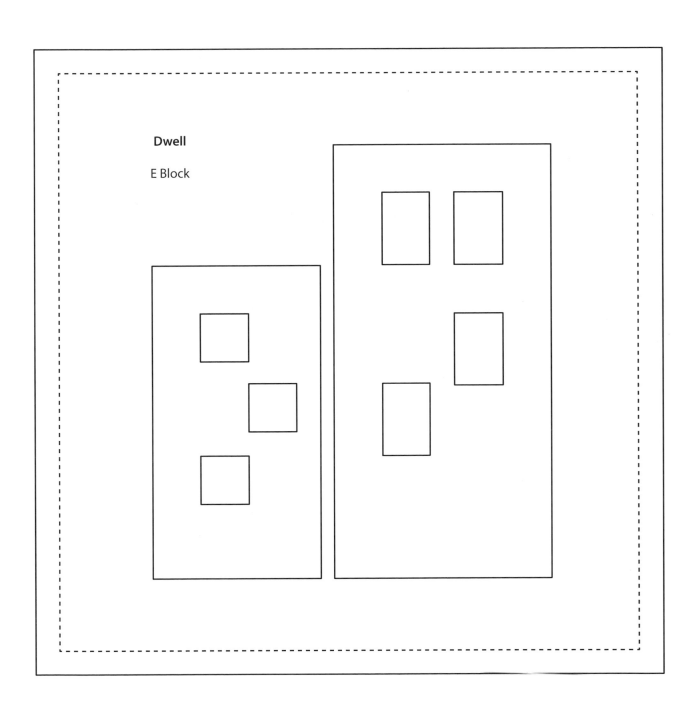

Dwell

E Block

THRIVE

FINISHED TABLE RUNNER / WALLHANGING: 18½″ × 36½″

Free flowing vines, leaves, and pomegranates are the focus of Thrive. This project can be used as a table runner but would be lovely as a vertical wallhanging as well. The wool in a variety of greens and reds looks beautiful on either a low-volume or dark print background and you can feature a different side-sashing fabric to complement your own decor.

Materials

If you want your project to be entirely scrappy without repeating prints, use the highest number of suggested prints in the range and make sure all pieces are at least the minimum size.

Low-volume or dark prints:

• 20–36 assorted 1½″ strips, minimum 12″ length

• 2 strips 2½″ × 12″

Or use alternate single-fabric background option: ⅜ yard.

Sashing fabric: ½ yard

Wool:

• 6–8 pieces (6½″ × 8″ each) in a variety of red, orange, pink, magenta, rust, and bright green

• 1 piece (13″ × 8″) in a second green for leaves and vines

Wool scrap: Light pink for berries

Backing fabric: ¾ yard

Batting: 23″ × 41″

Project Particulars

For my project as shown, I used felted wool from Local Farm Girl (see Resources, page 126) in the 03 and 04 ranges of the following colors: Cosmos, Red Lichen, Carrot, and Green Lichen. For the stitching, I used a simple running stitch (see Stitches, page 24) in either black or white 12-weight cotton thread.

Cutting

Low-volume or dark prints

• Cut 36 strips 1½″ × 12″ for center section.

• Cut 2 strips 2¼″ × 12″ for infinity-edge binding.

Alternate single-fabric option for center section

Cut in the order shown.

• Cut 1 rectangle 9½″ × 36½″.

• Cut 2 strips 2¼″ × 12″ for infinity-edge binding.

Sashing fabric

• Cut 3 strips 2¼″ × width of fabric for binding.

• Cut 1 strip 3½″ × 36½″ for left sashing.

• Cut 1 strip 6½″ × 36½″ for right sashing.

Backing

• Cut 1 rectangle 23″ × 41″.

Construction

Seam allowances for piecing and construction are ¼" throughout.

PIECE THE BACKGROUND

If using the alternate single-fabric background, skip to Prepare the Appliqué Pieces (next page).

1. Arrange the 36 strips 1½" × 12" in order of your liking.

2. Sew together along the long edges to make a strip set. Join the strips in pairs, then join the pairs, continuing until all 36 strips are joined in one large strip set. Press the seams in any direction you prefer.

3. Trim the strip set so that it measures 9½" × 36½". Run a straight stitch slightly less than ¼" away from the edges down both long sides of the strip set. This will secure the seams for handling while stitching appliqué. Since the securing line is stitched slightly less than ¼" away from the edge, it will be hidden in the seam allowance when you add sashing fabrics. *fig A*

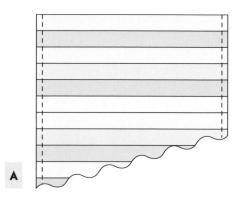

Piecing Skinny Strip Sets

When using skinny strips like the 1½" ones in the pieced background, there are a few things to keep in mind. With so many seams across the background, it is helpful to be careful to use a scant ¼", not a true ¼" seam. The scant ¼" is usually a couple of threads narrower and accommodates the fold in the fabrics once the piece is pressed. A true ¼" will create small shortages after pressing the seam which, when multiplied over the length, will result in a background that measures shorter than intended. Also, be sure to press the seams completely open to get the full expanse of the fabric between the seams.

PREPARE THE APPLIQUÉ PIECES

1. Follow the general directions in Appliqué Basics (page 22) to prepare your appliqué pieces.

2. Once fusible web has been applied to all wool selections and scraps, cut a 6″ square from the green wool (13″ × 8″) and follow the instructions in Bias-Cut Vines (below) to make the vines.

3. Prepare the number of pieces indicated on the patterns (see Thrive Patterns, page 125).

Bias-Cut Vines

Narrow strips cut from wool on the bias will give you flexible vines that can bend and curve throughout a design.

1. For enough vine pieces for Thrive, cut the prepared 6″ square of green wool the square in half, corner to corner.

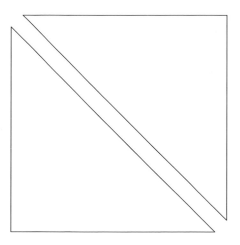

2. Cut ¼″ strips from the diagonal edges of both halves. If following my layout exactly, you will need to cut a total of 6 strips, 3 from each side of the initial cut.

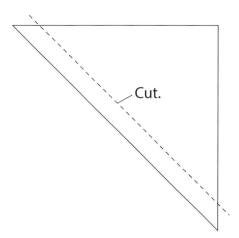

Cut.

PROJECT ASSEMBLY

1. Place the wool appliqué pieces on the pieced background. Use the diagram for help with placement. I found it best to arrange the vines first and then add the leaves and other elements. For help with appliqué placement of the curved vines, bend the vine pieces to your liking and pin into place temporarily as you arrange the other elements. *fig B*

2. When you are satisfied with the placement, fuse the wool pieces to the background.

3. Hand stitch as desired.

4. Sew the magenta or teal 36½″ strips to the long sides of the appliquéd panel; the narrow one to the left, the wider one to the right.

FINISHING

Layer and quilt as desired. For binding instructions, refer to Infinity–Edge Binding (page 124).

B

Thrive table runners or wallhangings, collaborative quilting with Tracey Fisher

Collaborative Quilting: Free-Motion and Wavy Echo with the Walking Foot

For the quilting on this project, I collaborated with longarm quilter, Tracey Fisher. With a chalk pencil, I first marked a gentle wavy line down the length of the appliqué on both sides. This gave Tracey a guideline for the inner part of free-motion quilting and also determined what would later be my first line of walking-foot quilting. Tracey completed the free-motion quilting design in the center of the project, outlining the appliqué pieces and adding detail in the center section.

After Tracey's center quilting was done, she added basting stitches to the sides where I was going to add the walking-foot quilting. You could also opt for adding a bit of basting spray between the layers on both sides. You may need to re-mark the gentle wavy line down the length of the appliqué on both sides if the chalk pencil wore off before continuing with the walking-foot quilting.

Select and use one of your presser feet that measures approximately ½″ from the edge to the needle. Using a presser foot with this approximate measure is the best way to achieve this design without having to mark every quilting line. If you want to change the density of quilting to a narrower or wider quilting line, you can just select a different-size foot to accommodate the wavy echo motif.

However, if you don't have a foot that gives you the spacing that you want, you can mark each wavy line as needed. The trick is to make the first line wavy enough that the curves won't flatten out as you go but not so tight that you can't stitch in a continuous line with the walking foot. Think of a letter S that has been stretched out a bit so the curves aren't so tight.

Feed the quilt top into the machine with the 6″ sashing side on the right and the center section and 3″ sashing side out to the left of your machine. With the walking foot on your domestic machine, first stitch the length of the project directly on the marked line, continuing out into the extra batting area.

When you get an inch or so out into the batting, with the needle down, pivot the piece right 90° and stitch over toward the outer edge of sashing for 4 or 5 stitches. With the needle down, pivot again, turning the piece another 90°. You'll now be heading back in the other direction without cutting the thread.

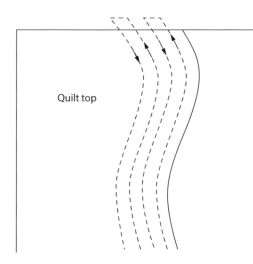

Quilt top

On the next pass, echo the first stitched wavy line, aligning the right side of your presser foot with the previous stitched curvy line. At the end of the next pass, again continue your stitches into the batting area. Needle down, pivot, this time to the left. Stitch over 4 or 5 stitches, needle down, and pivot left again to come back the other direction. This time the left side of your presser foot will align with the previously stitched line. Continue in this way, back and forth until the whole first side is completely quilted.

As your stitching line reaches the sides of the quilt top, continue to stitch off into the batting in a continuous stitching line. After the first pass off into the side batting, fill in the smaller curved sections in segments, cutting the thread between passes to fill out the remainder of the curve.

Repeat the process for the other side of sashing. Finally, trim the completed quilt top to 18½″ × 36½″. All the extra stitches out into the batting where you did your turnarounds will disappear in the trimming.

Infinity-Edge Binding

Like the name suggests, infinity-edge binding lets the quilt design continue over the edges without being broken up by a solid edge. This requires a change in binding strips as you go along to match your quilt top. It is easy to do.

For more detailed information on binding, see Basic Binding Instructions (page 27).

1. Prepare your binding colors separately. First, prepare and join all the binding strips that match the sashing fabric. This will be joined in one long piece initially.

2. Separately, prepare the 12″ binding strips that match the center background and set them aside.

3. Begin by attaching the sashing-matching, prepared binding in the middle of one of the long sides. *fig A*

4. Turn the corner as you normally would and continue for about an inch. Cut the thread and remove from the machine.

5. Take the piece over to your cutting surface. Lay the binding along the project edge until it meets the seam of the center section. Measure ¼″ beyond that seam and cut the binding strip at a straight angle. *fig B*

6. Join 1 of the 12″ binding strips by folding the project out of the way and sewing binding to binding with a straight seam. Press the seam in either direction.

7. Pin the newly joined binding in place where the seams align. Return to your machine and continue to attach the binding from where you left off. When you are about 4″–6″ before the second seam where center and sashing meet, cut the thread and remove from the machine. *fig C*

8. Repeat Steps 5 and 6, but this time to reattach the sashing binding strip, again at a straight angle.

9. Continue to attach the binding around the full project. Repeat Steps 4–8 at the other end of the table runner.

10. Complete binding as you normally would.

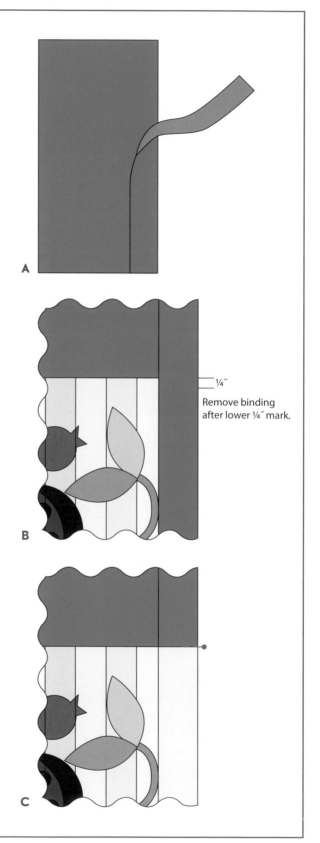

A

B

¼″

Remove binding after lower ¼″ mark.

C

Thrive

Berries
C1

C2

C3

Thrive

Large leaf
D1

THRIVE PATTERNS

	Pattern	Quantity
Pomegranate	A1	4
	A2	3
	A3	11
Pomegranate bud	B4	4
Berries	C1	4
	C2	5
	C3	4
Large leaf	D1	8
Medium leaf	D2	6
Layered leaves	D3	4
	D4	4

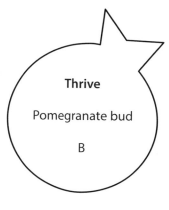

Thrive

Pomegranate bud

B

Thrive

Medium leaf

D2

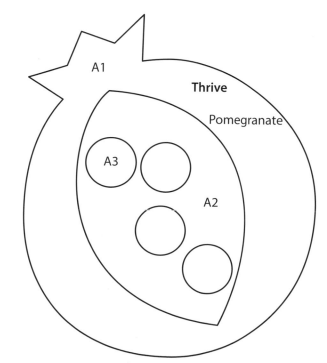

A1

Thrive

Pomegranate

A3

A2

D3

Thrive

Layered
leaves

D4

RESOURCES/BIBLIOGRAPHY

PROJECT KITS

Tonya Alexander   stashlabquilts.com

Limited project kits, wool bundles, and notions

WOOL

Local Farm Girl   localfarmgirl.com

Andover Fabrics   andoverfabrics.com

National Nonwovens   nationalnonwovens.com

BOOKS AND WEBSITES

Albers, Josef. *Interaction of Color: 50th Anniversary Edition*.
New Haven, CT: Yale University Press, 2013.

Goldsmith, Becky. *The Quilter's Practical Guide to Color*.
Lafayette, CA: C&T Publishing, Inc., 2015.

St. Clair, Kassia. *The Secret Lives of Color*.
New York: Penguin Books, 2017.

White, Sarah E. "Wool Allergy or Sensitivity?"
The Spruce Crafts, 12/13/2019.
thesprucecrafts.com > *search* "wool allergy" >
click "Knitting: Wool Allergy or Sensitivity?"

ABOUT THE AUTHOR

Tonya Alexander is a quiltmaker, designer, and all-out fabric lover. She didn't set out to be a quilter; she just wanted to make one quilt for a home decorating project. Fortunately, she discovered her love of fabric and all things scrappy and she has never looked back.

Her designs have appeared in publication in her first book, *Stash Lab*, and in many quilt and craft magazines including *American Patchwork & Quilting*, *Quilts and More*, *Simply Moderne* and *Simply Vintage* (both from *Quiltmania*), *McCall's Quilting* magazine, *Modern Patchwork* magazine, *Primitive Quilts and Projects*, and more.

Tonya lives in the Pacific Northwest with her family and travels to teach and share her love of quilting with others as much as she can. The PNW is blessed with more shades of green and good quilting days than she ever imagined.

Visit Tonya online and follow on social media:

Website: stashlabquilts.com

Instagram: @stashlabquilts

Facebook: Tonya Alexander Quilts